AACRAO

1910

AACRAO's
RETENTION
OF RECORDS

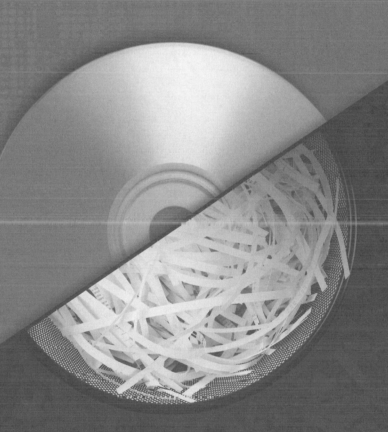

Guide for Retention and Disposal
of Student Records

AMERICAN ASSOCIATION OF COLLEGIATE REGISTRARS AND ADMISSIONS OFFICERS

AACRAO's

RETENTION OF RECORDS

Guide for Retention and Disposal
of Student Records

AACRAO®

American Association of Collegiate
Registrars and Admissions Officers
One Dupont Circle, NW, Suite 520
Washington, DC 20036–1135

Tel: (202) 293–9161 | Fax: (202) 872–8857 | www.aacrao.org

For a complete listing of AACRAO publications, visit www.aacrao.org/publications.

The American Association of Collegiate Registrars and Admissions Officers, founded in 1910, is a nonprofit, voluntary, professional association of more than 10,000 higher education administrators who represent more than 2,600 institutions and agencies in the United States and in 28 countries around the world. The mission of the Association is to provide leadership in policy initiation, interpretation, and implementation in the global educational community. This is accomplished through the identification and promotion of standards and best practices in enrollment management, information technology, instructional management, and student services.

AACRAO adheres to the principles of non-discrimination without regard to age, color, handicap or disability, ethnic or national origin, race, religion, gender (including discrimination taking the form of sexual harassment), marital, parental or veteran status, or sexual orientation.

LIBRARY OF CONGRESS CATALOGING-IN-PUBLICATION DATA

Retention of records.
AACRAO's retention of records : guide for retention and disposal of student records / prepared by The Committee on AACRAO's Retention of Records — 2010 update.

p. cm.

Includes bibliographical references.

ISBN 978-1-57858-091-0

1. College student records—United States.
2. Records retention—United States.
I. American Association of Collegiate Registrars and Admissions Officers.
II. Title.
III. Title: Retention of records.

LB2845.7.R48 2010
378.1'61—dc22
2009052911

Contents

CHAPTER **1**

Student Records Retention and Disposal 1

CHAPTER **2**

Developing a Records Retention and Disposal Program 5

CHAPTER **3**

Retention Schedule Recommendations 11

CHAPTER **4**

Methods of Storage 27

CHAPTER **5**

Security of Student Records 33

CHAPTER **6**

Policy Development for Academic Departments: Grand Valley State University Case Study 41

APPENDICES

Acknowledgments

Prepared by: The Committee on AACRAO's
*Retention of Records: Guide for Retention and
Disposal of Student Records* 2010 Update.

COMMITTEE MEMBERS

Member	Member Position/Organization	
V. Shelby Stanfield (Chair)	Registrar	The University of Texas at Austin
Richard Backes	Senior Associate Registrar	Washington State University (Pullman, WA)
Julie Ferguson	Assistant Dean for Student Affairs/Registrar	University of Medicine & Dentistry–New Jersey Medical School (Newark, NJ)
Martha Henebry	Director, Membership and Publications	AACRAO
Wendy Kilgore	Dean of Enrollment Services	Colorado Community College System (Denver, CO)
Jerry Montag	University Registrar	Grand Valley State University (Allendale, MI)
Robert Morley	Associate Registrar	University of Southern California (Los Angeles, CA)
Susan Nelson	University Registrar	University of Medicine & Dentistry (Newark, NJ)
Charles Toomajian	Registrar and Associate Dean of the College	Williams College (Williamstown, MA)
Susan Van Voorhis	Director of Academic Support Resources and University Registrar	University of Minnesota–Twin Cities (Minneapolis, MN)

Introduction

by **V. Shelby Stanfield, Registrar, The University of Texas at Austin**

Retention of Records. A Guide for Retention and Disposal of Student Records was first published in 1960. The *Guide* has been updated periodically as records management practices and requirements have changed and evolved. The first update (the 1979 edition) included recommended guidelines for the retention and disposal of specific hard copy documents, which proved to be invaluable information for records managers faced with sorting through a myriad of documents and deciding which to keep and which to discard.

The 1987 edition addressed issues related to the retention of records stored on microfilm and microfiche; on such computer media as tapes, disks, and diskettes; and optical disks. It was clear that more and more institutions relied on such media for record security and storage. In fact, hard copy records were being replaced by various computer media and records managers faced a new set of problems. Provisions had to be made for accessing, updating, displaying, securing, preserving, translating, transmitting, and converting data stored in machine-readable form. Managers of student records needed to be aware of the issues involved and insist on policies and procedures that ensured both the usefulness and the security of data stored in machine-readable form.

III

The 1987 *Guide* discussed the archival significance of student records. It was becoming clear that those records are important to genealogists, statisticians, historians, and posterity long after the students have left the institution. Archivists must select and preserve records and data that will convey a sense of the institution's past and contribute to significant research efforts. Records managers have some responsibility to the researchers and archivists of the future. This updated guide included recommendations for fulfilling this responsibility.

The 1987 *Guide* also provided reasonable standards to assist student records managers in making record retention decisions. Records retention and disposal practices should be as consistent as possible among colleges and universities. It represented the collective efforts of the American Association of Collegiate Registrars and Admissions Officers (AACRAO) Records Retention Task Force, the Records Management Committees, and a sample of the AACRAO members who responded to a questionnaire.

The 1998 edition acknowledged the technological advances that have created new options for records managers, especially electronic storage of records. It focused on updating financial aid and international student record requirements and state policies for records storage for schools that have closed. AACRAO continues to provide this information for professionals and others involved in records retention and disposal.

The 2000 edition had three primary objectives: i) to ensure that institutional records managers were aware of and compliant with new federal requirements for records administration, ii) to promote commonality in retention practices and policies used across institutions, and iii) to provide guidelines driven by technological changes.

The 2010 edition provides numerous updates throughout the guide. Chapter 3 has been expanded to provide additional information regarding recommendations for record retention schedules including differentiated retention periods for four-year schools and community and technical colleges. In addition, a case study that outlines developing a recommended policy for academic department offices on records retention and disposal has been added as Chapter 6. Given the complexity of record retention laws, Appendix E has been crafted to provide contact information for state records management agencies.

Technology continues to give records managers options such as CD-ROM, Optical Disk, Digital Versatile Disk (DVD) computer hard drives and related magnetic media as well as integrated circuitry media such as flash drives; all presenting greater storage capacity with each passing year. In addition, records managers have been given options such as data warehousing, sophisticated web tools, the Internet and workflow concepts to aid in distributing more efficient services firsthand to students, faculty, staff, parents and alumni. Electronic Data Interchange (EDI), eXensible Markup Language (XML) and Portable Document Format (PDF) have enabled institutions to send transcripts and other educational documents electronically. The fax machine continues to be used to transmit documents and we see a growing number of online systems; both developed by institutions in-house as well as offered by corporate partner service providers. Kiosks and labs around campuses and personal laptops make it easy for students to look up information and, in many cases, make changes. Telephones and Web sites have brought application, registration and grade reporting into the new age. Paper management and paper storage are no longer the primary concerns of a records retention policy. Chapter 4 of the 2010 *Guide*, Methods of Storage, considers storage media of records and provides a discussion of issues to consider for each of these storage media and formats as well as related policy and procedure considerations.

Currently, most institutions are using electronically generated records, many without a plan for destruction, retention, and recovery. Since information is so easily accessible and storage is seemingly limitless, it is hard to think of destroying or purging any of it. In time, however, computer mainframe disks and related storage technologies will soon present the same storage problems as filing cabinets have in the past and computer programs will become bogged down with information that should be archived or simply destroyed. Not all information needs to be preserved and traditionally has not been. In addition, with the heightening concern regarding privacy, it is critical that institutions destroy or purge information according to a set retention schedule based on institutional policy and federal and State law.

Most institutions are beginning to think of information in three categories:
- Online information that is used daily;
- Nearline information that needs to be accessible but is not often accessed; and
- Offline information that is rarely accessed but must be preserved.

It is the storage of near-line and offline information that must be addressed. However, it is equally important to ensure that offline information can be brought back online and accessed when needed. Institutions need to ensure that their off-line and online technologies and systems are compatible.

With auditors and external sources demanding "accountability," increasing numbers of registrars and records managers are finding themselves with no alternative but to invest in new technologies that support their evolving record retention issues and business continuity plans.

As more offices use electronic systems, the matters of security, records storage, backup and business continuity, recovery procedures and staff training become new challenges. In addition, poorly designed information systems and business processes, no matter how technologically advanced, can create nightmares when one has to access one record out of potentially thousands of daily computer transactions.

New challenges now confront records managers on how documents are to be classified, what level of security they are to have, and who within their institutions should be permitted to view each document. Some perceive security of the electronic records to be a problem because of the continuing growth of malware, data breaches and online attacks by hackers. Information systems and business processes and procedures must be designed with and include appropriate security precautions to avoid any unauthorized access or inadvertent data loss.

The 2010 *Guide* addresses these issues, placing greater emphasis on electronic records such as in the schedules found in Chapter 3 and in the expanded recommendations regarding the security of those records detailed in Chapter 5. Records management will be vital in the digital age, and future revisions of the Guide will be needed to address the rapid technological developments in the storage, security and retention of institutional records.

CHAPTER 1

Student Records Retention and Disposal

by **Wendy Kilgore, Dean of Enrollment Services, Colorado Community College System (Denver, CO)**

Historically, college and university records managers have been charged with the responsibility for appropriate student records retention and disposal practices. The Family Educational Rights and Privacy Act of 1974, as amended (FERPA) and subsequent amendments, however, initiated new public concern about Records management practices, which resulted in changes in federal, state, and local laws and regulations. These statutory innovations, coupled with socio-cultural developments, have increased the potential for direct or indirect institutional involvement in litigation. Unfortunately, the new regulations have not included instructions on how an institution and its managers can best comply with the new requirements.

Determining which records to keep and which not to keep is made more difficult by vague language in some laws and regulations. Records managers must maintain a balance between extremes of risk from the retention of everything to the disposal of the vital. The best guidelines for maintaining this balance are some basic principles to which good judgment can be applied.

1

Principles Governing Records Retention and Disposal

- Records retention policies, procedures and disposal programs should be developed to comply with institutional policy, as well as local, state, and federal laws.
- Records retention policies and procedures for any particular record type must be consistent.
- Records that identify a person are more subject to direct legal action than statistical or generic records; therefore, retention and disposal of these records require priority attention.
- Records that have been contested should never be destroyed unless the ability to reconstruct them in legally acceptable form is preserved. The destruction of permanent records should cease once litigation commences.
- Records for which there is no legally specified period for retention should be disposed of systematically in accordance with the institution's record retention and disposal program.
- Retention and disposal policies should include provisions for machine-readable records that can be accessed only with specific technology (unique computer hardware or software, etc.).
- Records retention and disposal policies, procedures and programs should be reviewed periodically and modified as mandated by changing legal requirements and institutional policy.
- Records retention policies, procedures and programs must take into consideration the longterm historical value as well as the accessibility of records.

Federal Laws and Regulations

Effective records managers keep themselves informed about federal laws and regulations pertaining to the maintenance, security, and retention of records. Monitoring of such laws and regulations should start with regular reference to the *Federal Register* and aacrao publications. The federal agencies which administer those laws and regulations that impact directly upon the retention of student records include the United States Department of Education, the Veterans Administration (va), the United States Public Health Service (phs), the Internal Revenue Service (irs), The Family Policy Compliance Office (ferpa office) and the Department of State.

Some programs affected by the records retention regulations are listed in Table 1, on page 3.

The records retention and disposal schedules in Chapter 3 of this Guide reflect the record retention requirements of these programs. The requirements of some of them, especially financial aid programs, arise from the institutional need to support claims for federal payments. The specific records to be maintained for these purposes are detailed in the pertinent laws and regulations, a list of which appears in Appendix C. Readers of this Guide are reminded, however, that even at this time there are bills that have passed, that may be amended, or have implementation issues that are being resolved that will affect Records management practices (*e.g.*, Hope

Department	Programs
Department of Education	▪ Educational Information Centers Program ▪ Graduate Fellowship Programs ▪ Federal Family Education Loan ▪ Perkins Loan Program ▪ Pell Grant Program ▪ Federal Work Study Program ▪ Supplemental Educational Opportunity Grants (SEOG)
Veterans Administration	▪ Educational Assistance Programs for Veterans ▪ Education Training Programs ▪ GI Bill Program ▪ Post-Vietnam Educational Assistance Program ▪ Vocation Rehabilitation Program ▪ Post 9/11 Program
United States Public Health Service	▪ Health Professions Loans ▪ Nursing Student Loans
Department of State Programs	▪ Agency for International Development Programs ▪ Student (F-1) and Scholar (J-1) programs

Scholarship, Solomon Amendment, Student Right-to-Know and Campus Security Act). Record managers are advised to regularly monitor federal laws and regulations. FERPA, also referred to as the "Buckley Amendment", deserves special attention here because of its significant impact on Records management. Specifically, FERPA requires that each institution establish a written policy and statement of adopted procedures covering the privacy rights of students.

In addition, except for disclosures of institutionally defined "directory information," FERPA requires institutions to maintain records of requests and disclosures of information that contain personally identifiable information. Generally, FERPA dictates prudence in the retention of records whenever the availability, accuracy, or content has been contested.

Whereas federal laws provide for the confidentiality of records and their retention, many state laws mandate access to and disclosure of records under "public information" or "open records" laws. An institution's policy statement on student records should provide both compliance with such laws and protection for the institution from unwarranted requests for student information. Records managers should therefore also continually monitor state legislation that affects record-keeping policies.

CHAPTER 2

Developing a Records Retention and Disposal Program

by **Julie Ferguson, Assistant Dean for Student Affairs/Registrar, University of Medicine & Dentistry – New Jersey Medical School (Newark, NJ)**
and **Susan Nelson, University Registrar, University of Medicine & Dentistry (Newark, NJ)**

The principal component of a records retention and disposal program is the schedule. The schedule is a policy statement outlining a plan and timetable for the disposition of student records. It must meet the administrative, fiscal, legal, legislative, and historical/research needs of the institution. The retention and disposal program should also take into consideration each record's historical value, which may extend to sources external to the institution. Public institutions may have greater record retention and disposal obligations than private institutions based on their state-supported status.

The goals of an effective records retention program should be to:

- Ensure that all vital records are maintained securely for the appropriate amount of time;
- Save valuable resources, money, time, space, and staff;
- Articulate the definition of various record(s), the medium in which they might exist, and where records may be housed;
- Ensure that legal requirements are met prior to record disposal;

5

■ Ensure that information of administrative, fiscal, legal, legislative and historical/research value is available;

■ Ensure that records to be destroyed are incinerated or shredded under controlled conditions;

■ Preserve confidentiality;

■ Ensure that record information is readily available when students request access;

■ Ensure that machine-readable records remain accessible when computers and other technological devices are changed; and

■ Ensure that institutional officials are trained in record retention and disposal.

It is recommended that each institution develop and implement its own records retention and disposal program in accordance with standards outlined in this guide. This implementation can be accomplished in six stages:

① Identification of need

② Inventory of records

③ Appraisal and categorization of records

④ Creation and implementation of a retention and disposal schedule

⑤ Publication, dissemination and training on retention and disposal program

⑥ Ongoing review and modification of the program

Identification of Need

Institutional and management needs for the records in question must be established and delineated as completely as possible before those who assume the responsibility for the development and implementation of a re-

cords retention program attempt to address several basic questions:

■ What records exist?

■ Which records are worthy of retention?

■ Where are the records created?

■ How long should those records be retained?

■ In what medium should they be retained?

■ How much space will they occupy?

■ Where are they to be stored to ensure security?

■ Who is/should be responsible for them?

■ How are computerbased records to be retained and accessed?

■ What are the existing federal, state, or local statutes that might affect retention of specific records?

■ Who needs access to each type of record and with what frequency?

■ How quickly can record content be retrieved?

■ How quickly can records be duplicated or reconstructed?

■ What will be the impact following disposal of records?

■ What are the relationships to other records produced within the office or institution?

Inventory of Records

An inventory of student records is the process of recording the location and identification of all types of records. This inventory is critical as it provides the basis for a sound records retention and disposal program. It should be comprehensive and will require great effort and collaboration at the institution. The inventory should collect all information necessary for the identification of all student records required by law (such as FERPA and Title IX) and satisfy student and institutional needs, such as:

- Record name and storage location
- Record custodian
- Summary of record content
- Frequency of record reference and update
- Record volume
- Inclusive record dates
- Record medium
- Annual accumulation
- Filing method
- Identification of "official" or "record" copy
- Copy distribution (if any)

A standard form should be developed to record the inventory information. A suggested format appears in Appendix A.

Appraisal and Categorization of Records

A sound records retention program requires a realistic appraisal of student records with regard to the duration of their usefulness and their value to the institution and to others. The outcome of such an appraisal should include the following:

- Establishment of reasonable retention periods;
- Identification of records which can be destroyed immediately;
- Identification of records which can be stored more efficiently;
- Identification of records with lasting value that should be placed in the archives; and
- Identification of the technology necessary to access records or determination of the necessity to convert the records to an accessible form.

A set of appraisal standards should be created to determine the administrative, fiscal, legal, legislative, and historical/research value of each record. Vital records may exist across all of these values.

A record is deemed to have:

- **Administrative value** if it assists the responsible office in an academic institution to perform its current or future tasks, such as student records maintenance, academic advisement, grade assignment, record reconstruction, and other academic action.

  Examples of documents classified as administrative records are original admission applications, registration and drop/add forms, residency forms, faculty grade lists, changes of grade, requests for special grade or registration options, and enrollment histories.

- **Fiscal value** if the information pertains to the receipt, transfer, payment, adjustment, or encumbrance of funds, or if the record is required for a financial or other fiscally-oriented audit. Examples include tuition receipts, transcript and other miscellaneous fee receipts, and residency classification changes.

- **Legal value** if it contains evidence of legally enforceable obligations and rights of the institution and its students. Among records having legal value are those which contain critical information that may serve as the basis for legal decisions and options and documents established in compliance with the Family Educational Rights and Privacy Act of 1974, as Amended, state laws and regulations, Veterans Administration regulations, Internal Revenue Service policies, Health Insurance Portability and Accountability Act, etc. Outlined in Chapter 3, Retention Schedule Recommendations, are other laws that directly affect student records.

- **Legislative value** if it is a document that a state or local government agency requires an institution to retain. This may apply only to public, rather than private, institutions; but such requirements may be greater than recommendations of professional organizations or other advisory groups to which institutions may turn for guidance. The greater of the retention periods for any document where two or more exist should be honored.

- **Historical/Research value** if the record has enduring value beyond the needs of the originating or custodian's office. Each records manager has a professional responsibility to consider the future historical/research value of student records for historical, genealogical, and other research. In assuming this responsibility, records managers should work closely with the institu-

tion's archivist and become familiar with any state laws requiring the archival preservation (permanent retention) of certain records. It is understood that the "disposition" of a record may mean transfer to the archives for permanent preservation or destruction after a specified retention period. Among those considered in this group are enrollment records, grade records and distribution, demographic data, degrees awarded, and various statistical reports.

Creation and Implementation of a Retention and Disposal Schedule

When all records have been inventoried and classified, a schedule should be prepared which identifies each series (and documents included in each series) and specifies the manner and time of its disposition. Before publication and implementation of this schedule, legal review, state or local approval, if necessary, and official institutional sanction should be secured.

It may be advantageous to establish interim storage centers for some records if the schedule for disposition (archival preservation or destruction) extends to a period of infrequent use or reference. This determination should be made after comparing the relative cost of active storage as opposed to an interim site and the level of security there.

Confidential records no longer needing to be retained should be destroyed by incineration, shredding, or other appropriate means. Managers of student records may be held responsible for the inappropriate or unauthorized disclosure of information as a consequence of improperly destroyed records. Unless records are actually destroyed at the end of the specific retention periods, the retention and disposal schedule becomes ineffective and the institution increases the risk of litigation. Records managers should establish procedures to monitor compliance with the retention and disposal recommendations. Records kept beyond their expected disposal date can be requested or subpoenaed and cannot be disposed of once requested. This may increase an institution's exposure during litigation.

The recommendations in retention and disposal schedules in this guide encompass records that generally reside in the offices of admissions, financial aid, records, or the registrar. The recommended retention period specified for each document denotes that at the conclusion of the stated retention period the original and all copies, regardless of form, should be destroyed unless the original is to be placed in archives. Records designated as permanent should be forwarded to the institution's archives when the frequency of references for administrative purposes declines sufficiently so that immediate access is no longer warranted.

Publication, Dissemination and Training on Records Management

Once a record retention and disposal program has been approved and a schedule established, institutions have an obligation to publish these documents in whatever format deemed appropriate to ensure that all record holders/custodians are aware of and can reference them on a regular basis. This can be a Web site, procedure manual, training guide, etc. This dissemination is critical to an effective program and helps to ensure a greater level of compliance across the institution. Once published and disseminated, staff should be trained on the program's requirements and retrained as it changes. Records management can be a component of new employee orientation, a topic of periodic training in custodial offices, annual compliance training, or as-needed based on institutional demands. Once trained, staff should receive certification documents and it is suggested that a centralized database of individuals who have completed training sessions be maintained by the Records Policy Committee (see below).

Review and Modification of Program: The Role of a Records Policy Committee

To remain effective, it is recommended that a review of records retention and disposal programs occur on an annual basis, or, at a minimum, at least once every three years. It is possible, for example, that the retention of a particular record deemed essential yesterday may be unnecessary today. A major change in information technology (such as a change from manual to an automated system or replacement of a computer system) also requires review of records retention policies. Additionally, institutions should be aware of and remain familiar with all state or local record retention and disposal regulations to which they are bound. (See Appendix E for links to each state's records management/archive department.)

To assure systematic monitoring and modification of the records program, it is recommended that a records policy committee be established and charged with that responsibility. If the records program is sufficiently comprehensive to include records other than those typically maintained by registrars, admissions, and financial aid officers, the committee membership should be appropriately representative. Some examples of stakeholders who would constitute the committee are the Office(s) of: Academic Affairs, Financial Aid, Bursar, Diversity/Minority Affairs, Student Affairs, Career Advisement, Faculty Affairs, Student Services, Information Technology, Library, Housing, Public Safety, Marketing, Alumni Affairs, Learning Center, etc. The institution's archivist should always be a member of the committee (see Appendix B, the Sample Institutional Records Policy).

Another model for monitoring the records program is the creation of an institutional Records Officer that is charged with ensuring the timely creation, review and approval of both departmental and institutional retention schedules. This central position would have jurisdiction to make recommendations for records retention and would coordinate approval by various entities, offices and state committees, as appropriate.

Institutional Closing

In the event that an institution of higher education ceases operations, it is the responsibility of the institution and the records managers to see that student records are moved to a location available to former students and that the students are properly notified of that location and the procedure necessary to obtain official transcripts as needed.

A comprehensive review of all records needed for fiscal and legal closure should also be made and provided to the administration or to the agency supervising the disposal of the charter and property.

The AACRAO publication *Transfer Credit Practices of Designated Educational Institutions* (TCP) is an excellent source of information on name changes of institutions, closing dates of institutions no longer in existence, and addresses for requesting records from those institutions. The records managers of the closing institution and the records managers assuming the responsibility for the permanent records should provide this information to the TCP reporting officer or officers if more than one state is involved.

Additional agencies that should be informed include the umbrella organization for higher education in the state, the information officer for the state legislature, and, in the case of private institutions, the sponsoring organization. See Appendix D, Policies Covering Disposition of Academic Records of Closed Schools.

CHAPTER 3

Retention Schedule Recommendations

by **Richard Backes, Senior Associate Registrar, Washington State University (Pullman, WA)**
and **Robert Morley, Associate Registrar, University of Southern California (Los Angeles, CA)**

The following recommended retention schedules are provided as resources for professionals in registrar, admissions, recruitment, financial aid offices and enrollment managers to assist in the development and maintenance of their respective schedules. While each example schedule may not include all records which student records managers may need to maintain, they are meant to reflect some of the most common records across these disciplines.

Moreover these retention schedules may contain several records series that are neither required nor useful for some institutions. Some schedules indeed may contain records for which an institution has found no need to retain and therefore are not meant to encourage the creation or retention of these records. Also, some of these retention recommendations may conflict with state laws and therefore should not be adopted in those states. Rather, the intent is to include the most conventional records with generic titles regardless of the medium in which they are maintained. A number of points should be stressed in considering these recommendations:

- In general, the recommendations are for minimum retention periods; some institutions may need to maintain certain records

11

for longer periods. When a recommendation is considered mandatory due to federal law or regulation, this will be explained in the notes section for that particular record series.

● To properly apply these recommendations it is necessary to identify the custodian of a particular record. For example, if the admissions applications of applicants who actually enter an institution are transferred from an admitting to a records office, the latter is deemed the custodian of those records whereas the former is the custodian of the applications of those who do not enter. Copies of original records held in offices other than the custodian's need not be retained beyond their use in those offices. Retention periods should be established for all copies of records to avoid excess accumulations of redundant records.

● If the retention period of a record exceeds five years beyond the "active" life of a record, and especially if the retention period is to be either indefinite or permanent, attention must be paid to the longevity and quality of the medium on which the record is stored as well as the availability of the technology necessary to maintain and access the record (*see* Chapter 4, Methods of Storage).

● An inventory of records may identify student records not specifically listed in this guide for which retention periods should also be established.

● The retention of documents and records beyond their scheduled retention can in-

crease risk of litigation, increase storage costs and staff time. In addition, the maintenance of records that are not listed in an institution's retention schedule poses risks for some of the same reasons. This includes all forms of the record.

● Records should be retained in the form that meets the administrative needs of the institution and any statutory or regulatory requirement. In some cases, this will necessitate that electronic records be maintained in electronic format. In other cases, paper records may be maintained in paper format or converted to an image for electronic storage. Public institutions should check relevant guidance from their state regarding retention of electronic records, including appropriate formats (some states require that records be retained in an ocular medium while other states leave the definition and medium of an official record as an institutional decision). Those institutions with imaging systems should also consider long-term retention of records and the implications of the chosen technology. For more information, see Chapter 4.

How to Use the Recommended Retention Schedules

There are two ways to find a particular record or document. First, the index below lists records/documents alphabetically and the associated schedule(s) where they are housed.

Second, the Retention Schedule Recommendations that follow are organized by broad category of record. It begins with

Schedule A related to applicant data and documents for those that do not enroll, and its close counterpart Schedule B for those applicants who do enroll and attend the institution. Schedules C contains the bulk of academic records related to a student's attendance and will be of most interest to Registrars. Schedule D is a new schedule meant to address the retention and disposal of electronic records, often found in student information systems and may be managed separately from office documents and data. Schedule E lists institutional reports and statistics typically published and/or maintained by schools. FERPA-covered data and records are listed separately in Schedule F while Schedule G lists federally-mandated disclosure records that must be maintained by institutions. Finally, Schedule H lists federal student financial aid requirements for retention.

Each schedule is organized alphabetically by section, if sections are utilized to organize the data. For example, in Schedule C, one section deals with academic and attendance records while another section covers certification records. For each record series, a title, description and recommended schedule for retention is provided. Notes are included for some records series which are referenced in a separate column. While these schedules are recommended, longer or short periods may be required by your particular institution and/or state. Consultation with records officers or committees at your institution and possibly at the state level will assist in determining the most appropriate retention period.

Retention Schedule A

*ADMISSIONS RECORDS FOR
APPLICANTS WHO DO NOT ENROLL*

These record series represent those documents that are part of the Admissions file for undergraduate, graduate, professional and non-degree applicants who do not subsequently enroll, regardless of their admission status, including if they were denied admission. These files are normally destroyed within a shorter period of time since no permanent record of attendance is maintained. (*See* Table 2, on page 14.)

Retention Schedule B

*ADMISSIONS RECORDS FOR
APPLICANTS WHO ENROLL*

These record series represent those documents that are part of the Admissions file for undergraduate, graduate, professional and non-degree applicants who do subsequently enroll and are considered enrolled students. These files are generally retained for a longer period of time, at least throughout the academic career of the student and usually longer. These records form the basis for the admission, transfer credit and sometimes completion of the student's academic program, and therefore should be available for review. In addition, students may stop out for long periods of time and return to the institution for additional coursework. Often some of these documents may need to be reviewed upon readmission or graduation. (*See* Table 3, on page 15.)

13

TABLE 2: SCHEDULE A—ADMISSIONS RECORDS FOR APPLICANTS WHO DO NOT ENROLL

Record Series Title	Description	Recommended Retention Period*		Notes
		Four-year Colleges and Universities	Community and Technical Colleges	
Admission Documents				
Admission letters	Notices of admission, denial, waitlist notification	1 year AA	V	1
Correspondence, relevant		1 year AA	V	1
Waivers of rights of access (admissions)	Waiving right of access to admission letters of recommendation	UT	V	1, 2
Application Materials				
Applications for admission or re-admission	Admission application such as undergraduate, graduate, international, non-degree/special admittance	1 year AA	V	1
Credit by examination	Reports/scores on Advanced Placement, CLEP, PEP, etc.	5 years AG	V	1
Entrance examination reports/test scores	Standardized test scores, such as ACT/SAT, LSAT, MCAT, GRE, TOEFL	1 year AA	V	1
Medical records	Includes such things as immunization records	1 year AA	V	1
Letters of recommendation (admissions)		1 year AA	V	1
Military documents		1 year AA	V	1
Placement test records/scores		1 year AA	V	1
Residency classification forms		1 year AA	V	1
Test scores (other)		1 year AA	V	1
Transcripts (high school)		1 year AA	V	1
Transcripts (other colleges)		1 year AA	V	1, 3
International Student Documents				
Alien Registration Receipt Card	Evidence of admissibility as a permanent resident	1 year AA	1 year AA	1
DS-2019	Certificate of eligibility for J1 visa status (formerly IAP-66)	1 year AA	1 year AA	1
Employment Authorization (work permit), if granted		1 year AA	1 year AA	1
I-20	Certificate of eligibility for F-1 visa status	1 year AA	1 year AA	1, 4
I-94 Card (copy)	Document issued to nonimmigrants; also known as Arrival-Departure Record	1 year AA	1 year AA	1
Passport number		1 year AA	1 year AA	1
Statement of Educational Costs	Estimate of total school year costs	1 year AA	1 year AA	1
Statement of Financial Responsibility	Evidence of adequate financial resources	1 year AA	1 year AA	1

* **AA:** After Application; **AG:** After graduation or non-attendance; **UA:** Until admitted; **UT:** Until terminated; **V:** Variable (until administrative need is satisfied)

[1] Although the retention period recommended for the documents listed above is one year (for four-year colleges and universities), federal legislation, state statutes, or institutional policy may dictate otherwise. The federal legislation which governs these records is as follows:
  ■ The IRS requires that, for taxexempt status for private institutions, the records of applicants who apply and do not enter be retained for three years.
  ■ VA regulations require that all recruitment materials used in the previous 12 months be retained (see note 4 of Schedule C).
[2] Records for applicants who do not enter are not covered by FERPA. Any waiver would be in effect while the record is maintained.
[3] Some documents from institutions in other countries may be originals and therefore difficult or impossible for the applicant to replace. The records custodian may want to return these documents to the applicant rather than destroy them.
[4] I-20 hardcopy forms will become an electronic form with the release of SEVIS II, scheduled for 2010.

TABLE 3: SCHEDULE B—ADMISSIONS RECORDS FOR APPLICANTS WHO ENROLL
....

Record Series Title	Description	Recommended Retention Period*		Notes
		Four-year Colleges and Universities	Community and Technical Colleges	
Admission Documents				
Admission letters†	Notices of admission, denial, waitlist notification	5 years AG	V	1, 4
Admission letters (Special Program)			3 years AG	4
Correspondence, relevant		5 years AG	3 years AG or V	1, 4
Waivers of rights of access (admissions)	Waiving right of access to admission letters of recommendation	UT	3 years AG	1, 2, 4
Application Materials				
Applications for admission or re-admission	Admission application such as undergraduate, graduate, international, non-degree/ special admittance	5 years AG	3 years AG or V	1, 4
Credit by examination	Reports/scores on Advanced Placement, CLEP, PEP, etc.	5 years AG	3 years AG or V	1, 4
Entrance examination reports/ test scores	Standardized test scores, such as ACT/SAT, LSAT, MCAT, GRE, TOEFL	5 years AG	3 years AG or V	1, 4
Medical records	Includes such things as immunization records	5 years AG	3 years AG or V	1, 4
Letters of recommendation (admissions)		UA[2]	3 years AG or V	1, 4
Military documents		5 years AG	3 years AG or V	1, 3, 4
Placement test scores/reports		5 years AG	3 years AG or V	1, 4
Release from high school or Dual Enrollment forms			3 years AG or V	
Residency classification forms		5 years AG	3 years AG or V	1, 4
Test scores (other)		5 years AG	3 years AG or V	1, 4
Transcripts (high school)		5 years AG	3 years AG or V	1, 4
Transcripts (other colleges)		5 years AG	3 years AG or V	1, 4, 5
International Student Documents				
Alien Registration Receipt Card	Evidence of admissibility as a permanent resident	5 years AG	5 years AG	1, 4, 6
DS-2019	Certificate of eligibility for J1 visa status (formerly IAP 66)	5 years AG	5 years AG	1, 4, 6

* **AA:** After Application; **AG:** After graduation or non-attendance; **UA:** Until admitted; **UT:** Until terminated; **V:** Variable (until administrative need is satisfied)
† including those programs with a separate admission process from the general application

[1] The retention periods recommended above are based on the following:
  ■ The forms are maintained in individual student folders and are retained at least five years (three years for community and technical colleges) after date of graduation or semester and year of last attendance. Some schools may wish to keep this material permanently as storage allows
  ■ Uniform retention periods allow for the destruction of the entire application folder which will save time reviewing and sorting documents.
  ■ Essential data will be recorded on academic records retained permanently (see AACRAO's Academic Record and Transcript Guide 2003).
[2] FERPA states that letters of recommendation not accompanied by waivers and retained beyond their intended use may be viewed by the student. As a consequence, it is recommended that these letters be destroyed after admission of the student. Waivers of rights of access filed with letters of recommendations should be retained as long as the file is retained. Students who revoke their waivers of rights of access may not see letters of recommendation submitted during the time the waivers were in force.
[3] VA regulations state that the following student records must be retained for at least three years after termination of enrollment:
  ■ Previous education or training (transcripts from other colleges and source documents for other nontraditional credit).
  ■ Evidence of formal admission (acceptance letters). The regulations state that longer retention will not be required unless a written request is received from the General Accounting Office or the VA no later than 30 days prior to the end of the threeyear period
[4] Educational institutions participating in federal, state, and private programs of low-interest loans to students must retain student records of admission and placement for three years after graduation or withdrawal. In the event of an open audit, records must be retained until all questions are resolved.
[5] Some documents from institutions in other countries may be originals and therefore difficult or impossible for the applicant to replace. The records custodian may want to return these documents to the applicant rather than destroy them.
[6] No upper limit for international students on student visas. For exchange visitor visas, 3 years after graduation or date of last attendance/Permanent.
[7] I-20 hardcopy forms will become an electronic form with the release of SEVIS II, scheduled for 2010.

TABLE 3: SCHEDULE B—ADMISSIONS RECORDS FOR APPLICANTS WHO ENROLL

Record Series Title	Description	Recommended Retention Period*		Notes
		Four-year Colleges and Universities	Community and Technical Colleges	
Employment Authorization (work permit), if granted		5 years AG	5 years AG	1, 4, 6
I-20	Certificate of eligibility for F-1 visa status	5 years AG	5 years AG	1, 4, 6, 7
I-94 Card (copy)	Document issued to nonimmigrants; also known as Arrival-Departure Record	5 years AG	5 years AG	1, 4, 6
Passport number		5 years AG	5 years AG	1, 4, 6
Statement of Educational Costs	Estimate of total school year costs	5 years AG	5 years AG	1, 4, 6
Statement of Financial Responsibility	Evidence of adequate financial resources	5 years AG	5 years AG	1, 4, 6

* **AA:** After Application; **AG:** After graduation or non-attendance; **UA:** Until admitted; **UT:** Until terminated; **V:** Variable (until administrative need is satisfied)
† including those programs with a separate admission process from the general application

[1] The retention periods recommended above are based on the following:
- The forms are maintained in individual student folders and are retained at least five years (three years for community and technical colleges) after date of graduation or semester and year of last attendance. Some schools may wish to keep this material permanently as storage allows.
- Uniform retention periods allow for the destruction of the entire application folder which will save time reviewing and sorting documents.
- Essential data will be recorded on academic records retained permanently (see AACRAO's Academic Record and Transcript Guide 2003).

[2] FERPA states that letters of recommendation not accompanied by waivers and retained beyond their intended use may be viewed by the student. As a consequence, it is recommended that these letters be destroyed after admission of the student. Waivers of rights of access filed with letters of recommendations should be retained as long as the file is retained. Students who revoke their waivers of rights of access may not see letters of recommendation submitted during the time the waivers were in force.

[3] VA regulations state that the following student records must be retained for at least three years after termination of enrollment:
- Previous education or training (transcripts from other colleges and source documents for other nontraditional credit).
- Evidence of formal admission (acceptance letters). The regulations state that longer retention will not be required unless a written request is received from the General Accounting Office or the VA no later than 30 days prior to the end of the threeyear period.

[4] Educational institutions participating in federal, state, and private programs of low-interest loans to students must retain student records of admission and placement for three years after graduation or withdrawal. In the event of an open audit, records must be retained until all questions are resolved.

[5] Some documents from institutions in other countries may be originals and therefore difficult or impossible for the applicant to replace. The records custodian may want to return these documents to the applicant rather than destroy them.

[6] No upper limit for international students on student visas. For exchange visitor visas, 3 years after graduation or date of last attendance/Permanent.

[7] I-20 hardcopy forms will become an electronic form with the release of SEVIS II, scheduled for 2010.

Retention Schedule C

STUDENT ACADEMIC RECORDS

These record series represent the core academic and administrative documents relevant to the academic achievement of students. These documents include program records, registration and enrollment records, certification records and grade, transcript and graduation records. While some records must be retained permanently, such as the academic transcript, others may be destroyed within a shorter timeframe due to their transient nature, such as course drop and add records. Each institution should evaluate the value in each series and consider the impact of longer or shorter retention schedules for each series. (*See* Table 4, on page 17.)

TABLE 4: SCHEDULE C—STUDENT ACADEMIC RECORDS

Record Series Title	Description	Recommended Retention Period*		Notes
		Four-year Colleges and Universities	Community and Technical Colleges	
Academic Program Records				
Academic advisement records		2 years AG	3 years AG	2, 3, 5
Academic warning	Notice of academic action related to academic non-performance/deficiency	5 years AG	V	2, 3, 5
Academic suspension	(same as above)	5 years AG	3 years AG	2, 3, 5
Academic dismissal	(same as above)	P	3 years AG	3, 5
Academic integrity code violations (with sanctions)	Notice of violation of academic integrity policies including sanctions, if any	P	3 years AG	1, 3, 5
Academic Records (miscellaneous)	Narrative evaluations, competency assessments, etc.	P	PᴬA	1, 3, 5, 6
Correspondence (student)	Related to academic records, inquiries	1 year	3 years AG	3, 5
Disciplinary action records	Grade or program actions, notice of sanctions related to personal conduct	5 years AG	3 years AG	2, 3, 5
Grievance/complaint (by student)	Various course/exam related issues. Not grade or FERPA disputes (see Grade appeal/complaint or Schedule F)	3 years after closure	3 years AG	3, 5
Leave of Absence		2 years	V	3, 5
Major changes, Certification of 2nd Majors, Minors		5 years AG	V	2, 3, 5
Petitions (academic)	Exceptions to academic rules	4 years	3 years AG	3, 5

* **AA:** After Application; **AG:** After graduation or non-attendance; **CC:** After course completion; **CERT:** After certification; **DD:** After date distributed; **DS:** After date submitted; **P:** Permanent; **UA:** Until admitted; **UT:** Until terminated; **V:** Variable (until administrative need is satisfied)

ᴬ if college procedures require this to be a part of the academic transcript
ᴮ or pursuant to athletic association rules
ᶜ if work not returned to student
ᴰ or permanent if part of the institution academic transcript

[1] Any record recommended for permanent retention should be retained in a medium that takes into consideration the nature of the document and its need for retrieval (see Chapter 5, Methods of Storage).

[2] The recommended retention period based on graduation or non-attendance should begin with the date of graduation or the date, term, or semester and year of last attendance.

[3] FERPA specifically requires institutions to maintain records of requests and disclosures of personally identifiable information except for defined "directory information" and requests from students for their own records. The records of disclosures and requests for disclosures are considered part of the students' educational records; therefore, they must be retained as long as the education records to which they refer are retained by the institution (see Retention Schedule F).

[4] The VA regulations state that the following records must be retained for at least three years after termination of enrollment:
- Grade reports and/or statements of progress (academic records)
- Change of course forms
- Transfer credit evaluation
- Degree audit records

VA regulations require that all advertising, sales, and enrollment materials (e.g., catalogs) used by or on behalf of the institution during the previous 12 months must be retained and available for review. In addition, records of tuition and fees charged to and collected from students, grade reports and statements of progress (academic records), and previous education and training documents (transfer credit evaluations) must be retained for three years.

[5] Educational institutions that participate in federal, state, and private programs of lowinterest loans to students must retain for three years after graduation or withdrawal students' records of academic progress, attendance, and courses studied according to an amendment of the General Education Provisions Act amended by the Improving America's Schools Act of 1994 (Public Law 103382). In the event of an open audit, records must be retained until all questions are resolved.

In addition to keeping records of all financial aid the student receives, institutions will need a financial aid transcript for a transfer student.

[6] Although student records created and maintained by medical and dental schools are usually narrative assessments of academic progress or clinical practice, for purposes of this retention schedule, such records are in the same category as the academic record.

[7] The VA requires that all records and computations showing compliance with the requirements of the VA Regulation No. 14201 (the 8515 percent ratio of nonveteran/veteran students for each course) be retained for at least three years. Longer retention will not be required unless a written request is received from the VA not later than 30 days prior to the end of the three year period.

TABLE 4: SCHEDULE C—STUDENT ACADEMIC RECORDS

Record Series Title	Description	Recommended Retention Period*		Notes
		Four-year Colleges and Universities	Community and Technical Colleges	
Thesis/Dissertation		P	n/a	1, 3, 5
Transcripts	Permanent academic record	P	P	1, 3, 5
Certification/Verification Records				
Athlete Eligibility reports		1 year CERT	V[B]	3, 5
Athlete records	Initial and continuing eligibility information, academic information, documentation of participation, tutor evaluation and assessment	10 years	V[B]	3, 5
Enrollment verifications	Verifications of enrollment, graduation, GPA and other related academics	1 year after verification	V	3, 5
Residency verification records	Documents in support of verifying residency in state for tuition purposes	6 years after submission	V	3, 5
Teacher certifications		1 year CERT	V	3, 5
Transcript requests (student)	Official transcript requests by student	1 year DS	V	3, 5
VA certification records	Certifying documents for federal VA benefits	3 years AG	3 years AG	2, 3, 4, 5, 7
Degree and Certificate Records				
Application for degree or other credential	Degree application, record of degree name, etc	5 years AG	3 years AG or V	2, 3, 5
Degree audit records	Degree audits in support of graduation clearing	5 years AG	3 years AG	2, 3, 5

* **AA:** After Application; **AG:** After graduation or non-attendance; **CC:** After course completion; **CERT:** After certification; **DD:** After date distributed; **DS:** After date submitted; **P:** Permanent; **UA:** Until admitted; **UT:** Until terminated; **V:** Variable (until administrative need is satisfied)
[A] if college procedures require this to be a part of the academic transcript
[B] or pursuant to athletic association rules
[C] if work not returned to student
[D] or permanent if part of the institution academic transcript

[1] Any record recommended for permanent retention should be retained in a medium that takes into consideration the nature of the document and its need for retrieval (see Chapter 5, Methods of Storage).
[2] The recommended retention period based on graduation or non-attendance should begin with the date of graduation or the date, term, or semester and year of last attendance.
[3] FERPA specifically requires institutions to maintain records of requests and disclosures of personally identifiable information except for defined "directory information" and requests from students for their own records. The records of disclosures and requests for disclosures are considered part of the students' educational records; therefore, they must be retained as long as the education records to which they refer are retained by the institution (see Retention Schedule F).
[4] The VA regulations state that the following records must be retained for at least three years after termination of enrollment:
 ▪ Grade reports and/or statements of progress (academic records)
 ▪ Change of course forms
 ▪ Transfer credit evaluation
 ▪ Degree audit records

 VA regulations require that all advertising, sales, and enrollment materials (e.g., catalogs) used by or on behalf of the institution during the previous 12 months must be retained and available for review. In addition, records of tuition and fees charged to and collected from students, grade reports and statements of progress (academic records), and previous education and training documents (transfer credit evaluations) must be retained for three years.
[5] Educational institutions that participate in federal, state, and private programs of lowinterest loans to students must retain for three years after graduation or withdrawal students' records of academic progress, attendance, and courses studied according to an amendment of the General Education Provisions Act amended by the Improving America's Schools Act of 1994 (Public Law 103382). In the event of an open audit, records must be retained until all questions are resolved.

 In addition to keeping records of all financial aid the student receives, institutions will need a financial aid transcript for a transfer student.
[6] Although student records created and maintained by medical and dental schools are usually narrative assessments of academic progress or clinical practice, for purposes of this retention schedule, such records are in the same category as the academic record.
[7] The VA requires that all records and computations showing compliance with the requirements of the VA Regulation No. 14201 (the 8515 percent ratio of nonveteran/veteran students for each course) be retained for at least three years. Longer retention will not be required unless a written request is received from the VA not later than 30 days prior to the end of the three year period.

TABLE 4: SCHEDULE C—STUDENT ACADEMIC RECORDS

Record Series Title	Description	Recommended Retention Period*		Notes
		Four-year Colleges and Universities	Community and Technical Colleges	
Diplomas (returned)		5 years	V	3, 5
Graduation lists	Lists of graduates for graduating class	P	V	1, 3, 5
Substitution/ waivers	Approvals to meet program requirements with administrative action	5 years AG	3 years AG	2, 3, 5
Grade and Scholarship/Deficiency Records				
Exams (final)/graded coursework		1 year CCᶜ	1 year CCᶜ	3, 5
Grade appeal/complaint	Student final grade disputes	1 year	1 year	3, 5
Grade book (faculty)	Record of students in course and work completed	5 years CC	5 years CC	3, 5
Grade change forms	Record of authorization to change grade	5 years AG	3 years AG	2, 3, 5
Grade reports (final)	Record of grades released to students	1 year DD	1 year DD or V	3, 5
Grade reports (midterm)	Record of mid-term grades submitted by faculty	End of term	End of term	3, 5
Grade submission sheets/data	Original record of grades submitted at end of term	P	P	1, 3, 5
Miscellaneous Records				
Name change authorizations		5 years AG	V	2, 3, 5
Personal data information forms	Change of address, race/ethnicity questionnaires, other demographic data	1 year AG	V	2, 3, 5

ᴬ **AA:** After Application; **AG:** After graduation or non-attendance; **CC:** After course completion; **CERT:** After certification; **DD:** After date distributed; **DS:** After date submitted; **P.** Permanent; **UA.** Until admitted; **UT.** Until terminated; **V:** Variable (until administrative need is satisfied)
ᴬ if college procedures require this to be a part of the academic transcript
ᴮ or pursuant to athletic association rules
ᶜ if work not returned to student
ᴰ or permanent if part of the institution academic transcript

1 Any record recommended for permanent retention should be retained in a medium that takes into consideration the nature of the document and its need for retrieval (see Chapter 5, Methods of Storage).
2 The recommended retention period based on graduation or non-attendance should begin with the date of graduation or the date, term, or semester and year of last attendance.
3 FERPA specifically requires institutions to maintain records of requests and disclosures of personally identifiable information except for defined "directory information" and requests from students for their own records. The records of disclosures and requests for disclosures are considered part of the students' educational records; therefore, they must be retained as long as the education records to which they refer are retained by the institution (see Retention Schedule F).
4 The VA regulations state that the following records must be retained for at least three years after termination of enrollment:
 ■ Grade reports and/or statements of progress (academic records)
 ■ Change of course forms
 ■ Transfer credit evaluation
 ■ Degree audit records

 VA regulations require that all advertising, sales, and enrollment materials (e.g., catalogs) used by or on behalf of the institution during the previous 12 months must be retained and available for review. In addition, records of tuition and fees charged to and collected from students, grade reports and statements of progress (academic records), and previous education and training documents (transfer credit evaluations) must be retained for three years.
5 Educational institutions that participate in federal, state, and private programs of low-interest loans to students must retain for three years after graduation or withdrawal students' records of academic progress, attendance, and courses studied according to an amendment of the General Education Provisions Act amended by the Improving America's Schools Act of 1994 (Public Law 103382). In the event of an open audit, records must be retained until all questions are resolved.

 In addition to keeping records of all financial aid the student receives, institutions will need a financial aid transcript for a transfer student.
6 Although student records created and maintained by medical and dental schools are usually narrative assessments of academic progress or clinical practice, for purposes of this retention schedule, such records are in the same category as the academic record.
7 The VA requires that all records and computations showing compliance with the requirements of the VA Regulation No. 14201 (the 8515 percent ratio of nonveteran/veteran students for each course) be retained for at least three years. Longer retention will not be required unless a written request is received from the VA not later than 30 days prior to the end of the three year period.

TABLE 4: SCHEDULE C—STUDENT ACADEMIC RECORDS

Record Series Title	Description	Recommended Retention Period*		Notes
		Four-year Colleges and Universities	Community and Technical Colleges	
Transfer credit evaluations		5 years AG	3 years AG[D]	2, 3, 5
Tuition and fee charges		5 years AG	3 years AG	2, 3, 5
Registration and Enrollment Records				
Class schedules (students)	Student schedules for each term	1 year AG	3 years AG	2, 3, 5
Class lists	Record of class rosters for each term	P	V	1, 3, 5
Course repeat form/approval		1 year DS	1 year DS	3, 5
Credit/no credit, audit, pass/no pass approvals	Authorizations for various enrollment options	1 year DS	V	3, 5
Enrollment Changes	Record of student add/drop/withdraw from class	1 year DS	V	3, 5
Hold or encumbrance authorizations	Registration and transcript holds	1 year after released	V	3, 5
Registration/Enrollment records	Initial registration forms, current enrollment records	1 year DS	V	3, 5
Withdrawal/cancellation of enrollment records	Record of request to withdraw from all classes	5 years AG	V	2, 3, 5

* **AA:** After Application; **AG:** After graduation or non-attendance; **CC:** After course completion; **CERT:** After certification; **DD:** After date distributed; **DS:** After date submitted; **P:** Permanent; **UA:** Until admitted; **UT:** Until terminated; **V:** Variable (until administrative need is satisfied)
[A] if college procedures require this to be a part of the academic transcript
[B] or pursuant to athletic association rules
[C] if work not returned to student
[D] or permanent if part of the institution academic transcript

[1] Any record recommended for permanent retention should be retained in a medium that takes into consideration the nature of the document and its need for retrieval (see Chapter 5, Methods of Storage).
[2] The recommended retention period based on graduation or non-attendance should begin with the date of graduation or the date, term, or semester and year of last attendance.
[3] FERPA specifically requires institutions to maintain records of requests and disclosures of personally identifiable information except for defined "directory information" and requests from students for their own records. The records of disclosures and requests for disclosures are considered part of the students' educational records; therefore, they must be retained as long as the education records to which they refer are retained by the institution (see Retention Schedule F).
[4] The VA regulations state that the following records must be retained for at least three years after termination of enrollment:
  ▪ Grade reports and/or statements of progress (academic records)
  ▪ Change of course forms
  ▪ Transfer credit evaluation
  ▪ Degree audit records

  VA regulations require that all advertising, sales, and enrollment materials (e.g., catalogs) used by or on behalf of the institution during the previous 12 months must be retained and available for review. In addition, records of tuition and fees charged to and collected from students, grade reports and statements of progress (academic records), and previous education and training documents (transfer credit evaluations) must be retained for three years.
[5] Educational institutions that participate in federal, state, and private programs of lowinterest loans to students must retain for three years after graduation or withdrawal students' records of academic progress, attendance, and courses studied according to an amendment of the General Education Provisions Act amended by the Improving America's Schools Act of 1994 (Public Law 103382). In the event of an open audit, records must be retained until all questions are resolved.

  In addition to keeping records of all financial aid the student receives, institutions will need a financial aid transcript for a transfer student.
[6] Although student records created and maintained by medical and dental schools are usually narrative assessments of academic progress or clinical practice, for purposes of this retention schedule, such records are in the same category as the academic record.
[7] The VA requires that all records and computations showing compliance with the requirements of the VA Regulation No. 14201 (the 8515 percent ratio of nonveteran/veteran students for each course) be retained for at least three years. Longer retention will not be required unless a written request is received from the VA not later than 30 days prior to the end of the three year period.

Record Series Title	Description	Recommended Retention Period*		Notes
		Four-year Colleges and Universities	Community and Technical Colleges	
Data change logs	Electronic log of changes to enrollment and other data, including date/time stamp information and user that changed data if that data is maintained separately in system	10 years	V[A]	
E-mail data/information	E-mails and other electronic communications that authorize academic/enrollment actions and/or provide directory/non directory information about a student	V[B]	V	1
Enrollment data	Electronic record of enrollment in classes, including records of drop, add and enrollment change activity	10 years	V[A]	
Grade data	Electronic record of submitted grades and grade changes, including date/time stamp and user data	P	V[A]	
Student demographic information	Electronic student data including student characteristics, date of birth, former names, address information, photo ID and ethnic information, etc.	50 years	V[A]	2

* **P:** Permanent; **V:** Variable (until administrative need is satisfied)
[A] or until the records retention requirement for the associated student record component is met (whichever is longer)
[B] based on content of e-communication

[1] E-mail regarding student records that are transitory in nature can be discarded when no longer needed. E-mail and electronic communication that contains important information or that forms the basis or the results of an academic or administrative decision may need longer retention. Example: E-mail containing approval for a change of major would be retained according to the retention schedule for Major Changes in Schedule C. Consult other schedules for similar information to determine retention schedule.
[2] Student demographic data and other information about a student who has attended the institution will likely need to be kept for a much longer period and/or permanently.

Retention Schedule D

STUDENT RECORD ELECTRONIC DATA

This retention schedule addresses the retention of electronic data stored in student information systems, and how that schedule may be different than the records kept within an administrative office. While the other retention schedules may be applied to electronic records as well as to paper records, data contained in central computing systems may require additional consideration and coordination between central Information Technology staff and administrative offices. (*See* Table 5.)

Retention Schedule E

PUBLICATIONS, STATISTICAL DATA, AND INSTITUTIONAL REPORTS

These record series are examples of typical reports and statistics compiled at institutions. Some are mandatory based on specific legislation while others may be recommended.

Record Series Title	Description	Recommended Retention Period*		Notes
		Four-year Colleges and Universities	Community and Technical Colleges	
Catalogs	Published, annually or bi-annually, record of courses, degrees and programs of study offered.	P	P	1, 4
Commencement programs	Published record of graduates for public distribution.	P	V	1
Degree statistics	Record of degrees granted by institution per graduation term and/or annually.	P	V	1
Enrollment statistics	Per term report of enrolled students, e.g. by class, by course, totals, headcount and FTE.	P	V	1
Grade distribution and other grade statistics	Report of grades given including summary grade point statistics by class	P	V	1
Instructor evaluations (by students)		1 semester	V	1
Race/ethnicity reporting	Report of student enrollment, graduation and other metrics by race and ethnic origin	P	V	1, 2, 3
Schedules of classes	Per term listing of all courses offered including time/day and seat limits	P	V	1

* **P**: Permanent; **V**: Variable (until administrative need is satisfied)

[1] Any record recommended for permanent retention should be retained in a medium that takes into consideration the nature of the document and its need for retrieval (see Chapter 5, Methods of Storage).

[2] The IRS requires that private schools maintain records reflecting the racial composition of the student body, faculty, and administrative staff for each academic year, and retain such records for a period of three years beginning with the year after compilation or acquisition.

[3] Section 504 of the Rehabilitation Act of 1973 requires that institutions maintain the necessary information and accurate compliance reports in such form that the determination of whether or not an institution is in compliance could be easily ascertained. In addition, racial and ethnic data are required to show the extent to which members of minority groups are beneficiaries of and participants in federally assisted programs. There is no time limit specified in the law.

[4] The IRS requires that private schools retain copies of all admission and scholarship brochures, catalogs, and advertising materials for a period of three years beginning with the year after compilation or acquisition.

In all cases, reports, data and statistics should be retained in the format in which they are created. If a report is electronic, then the retention of the record is recommended to be electronic (see notes at beginning of this chapter). (*See* Table 6.)

Retention Schedule F

FAMILY EDUCATIONAL RIGHTS AND PRIVACY ACT (FERPA) RECORDS

These records relate to students' ability to consent to disclosure of their records and the right under FERPA to request amendment of their records. In addition, the requirement to document requests for and access to education records is addressed. (*See* Table 7, on page 23.)

Retention Schedule G

FEDERAL DISCLOSURE RECORDS

The statutory requirements of the Higher Education Opportunity Act of 2008 continue to require institutions to maintain and retain records developed in compliance with

TABLE 7: SCHEDULE F—FAMILY EDUCATIONAL RIGHTS AND PRIVACY ACT (FERPA) RECORDS

Record Series Title	Description	Recommended Retention Period*	Notes
Requests for formal hearings	Student-initiated request for formal hearing regarding amendment of education record	P[A]	2
Requests for and disclosures of personally identifiable information	Necessary for compliance with record-keeping requirements in FERPA	P[B]	1, 2
Requests for nondisclosure of directory information	Student request to opt-out of directory information disclosure	P or UT	3
Statements on content of records regarding hearing panel decisions	If student request for amendment of record not granted, then student statement is included in record	P[A]	
Written consent for records disclosure	Student signed (electronic or paper) authorization for disclosure of education record	P or UT	
Waivers for rights of access		UT[A]	2
Written decisions of hearing panels	Decisions resulting from formal hearings regarding amendment of education records	P[A]	

* **P:** Permanent; **UT:** until terminated by the student
[A] as long as the record is maintained
[B] as long as disclosed record is maintained

[1] Requests for disclosure and disclosure of personally identifiable information must be maintained with the records that were disclosed as long as the records are maintained. While disclosures with student consent and disclosures to other school officials are exempt from this requirement, many disclosures under the exceptions requiring student consent must be recorded. This list of disclosures must be provided to students upon request. For more on this requirement, see the latest edition of the AACRAO FERPA Guide.
[2] Whenever the recommended retention period is the life of the affected record, the retention period of the FERPA document is meant to be the same as that of the student records to which it pertains: students' waivers of rights to access to letters of recommendation, for example, should be retained until terminated or the letters themselves are destroyed (see Retention Schedules A and B). If the retention period for a record to which a FERPA document pertains is permanent, the FERPA document should also be permanently retained.
[3] Final FERPA regulations published in 2008 clarify that requests to "opt-out" of disclosing directory information must be honored for former students no longer in attendance unless terminated by the student.

the *Campus Crime, Student Right-to-Know* and *Athletic Participation/EADA* disclosure requirements. The records must generally be retained for 3 years subsequent to the required date of disclosure. Specific requirements follow. (*See* Table 8, on page 24.)

Retention Schedule H

FEDERAL STUDENT FINANCIAL AID (SFA) RECORD RETENTION REQUIREMENTS

The statutory requirements of the Higher Education Opportunity Act of 2008 continue

to require Title IV institutions to maintain and retain records developed in compliance with the *Campus Crime, Student Right-to-Know* and *Athletic Participation/EADA* disclosure requirements. See Schedule G for more information. These records must generally be retained for 3 years subsequent to the required data of disclosure. All retention periods are mandatory. (*See* Table 9, on page 25.)

23

Record Series Title	Description	Recommended Retention Period*	Notes
Athletic Participation/ EADA documents		3 years RD	1, 5
College Costs, Accreditation, Textbook Information, Transfer Credit Policy	Complies with the Higher Education Opportunity Act	3 years RD	1, 7
Crime Statistics/Security Reports	Complies with Clery Act reporting requirements	3 years RD	1, 2, 3
Graduation/Completion, Transfer-out Data	Complies with Student Right-to-Know legislation	3 years RD	1, 4
Institutional Information (Cost of Attendance, Withdrawal Procedures, Accreditation, etc.)		3 years RD[A]	1, 6

* **RD:** from date of required disclosure
[A] or end of award year

[1] All retention periods in this Schedule are mandatory.
[2] **Campus Crime/Security Records and Reports** must be established and disclosed annually to students and employees. The records should contain such information as: 1) institutional policies and proceedings for reporting crimes, 2) crime statistics, 3) description of drug and alcohol abuse education programs, policies concerning possession, use and sale of alcoholic beverages or drugs, 4) statement of sexual assault prevention programs, 5) statistics on number of arrests for violations of liquor, drug abuse, or weapons laws, 6) procedures for campus disciplinary actions for alleged sex offenses, and 7) statement of security and access policies for campus facilities.
[3] **Examples of Crime Records Requirements:** Crime records should be retained for a 3-year period following the date of disclosure; i.e., institutions are required to retain records to substantiate information in the reports released for 3 years. In practical terms, this means data included in the report that will be distributed (disclosed) to students and employees by October 1, 2000, should be retained for 3 years from October 1, 2000, as follows:
  ■ Calendar Year 1997 records—must be retained until October 1, 2003
  ■ Calendar Year 1998 records—must be retained until October 1, 2004
  ■ Calendar Year 1999 records—must be retained until October 1, 2005

[4] **Graduation/Completion and Transfer-out rates/SRK Disclosure records** should be established and disclosed annually to students and other required parties. Records should be retained for 3 years from the annual July 1st required disclosure date.
  ■ Example 1: Graduation, completion and/or transfer rate information that must first be disclosed by July 1, 2000 (e.g., by schools with the longest programs of 2 years) must be retained until July 1, 2003.
  ■ Example 2: Graduation, completion and/or transfer rates that must be disclosed by July 1, 2003 (e.g., by schools with the longest programs of 4 years) must be retained until July 1, 2006.

[5] **Athletic Participation/EADA records** should be established and disclosed annually to students and other required parties. Records should be retained as follows:
  ■ Example 1: Records created for the disclosure that is required by October 15, 2000, must be retained until October 15, 2003.
  ■ Example 2: Records created for the disclosure that is required by October 15, 2001, must be retained until October 15, 2004.

[6] **Types of Institutional Information** that must be disclosed to students annually are listed below. The records should minimally be retained for 3 years from the date of disclosure. They include: 1) requirements and procedures for withdrawing from the institution, 2) cost of attendance (tuition/fees charges, books/supplies costs, room and board charges, related charges), 3) refund policy, 4) summary of requirements for return of Title IV grants or loans, 5) current academic programs of the institution (current degree programs, educational/training programs, faculty), 6) names of associations, agencies accrediting the institution, 7) description of special facilities and services for disabled students, 8) the school's policy on enrollment in study abroad programs, and 9) titles of persons to contact for information.
[7] Rules regarding the Higher Education Opportunity Act were not yet published as of this revision of the guide. More information can be found at http://www.ed.gov/policy/highered/leg/hea08/index.html.

TABLE 9: SCHEDULE H—FEDERAL STUDENT FINANCIAL AID (SFA) RECORD RETENTION REQUIREMENTS

Record Series Title/Description	Retention Period Minimal	Notes
SFA Program Records		
Accrediting and licensing agency review, approvals and reports	3 years AY	1, 2, 3, 4
Audit reports and school responses	3 years AY	1, 2, 3, 4
Records pertaining to financial responsibility and standards of administrative capability	3 years AY	1, 2, 3, 4
Program Participation Agreement	3 years AY	1, 2, 3, 4
Self-evaluation reports	3 years AY	1, 2, 3, 4
State agency reports	3 years AY	1, 2, 3, 4
SFA Fiscal Records		
Bank statements for accounts containing SFA funds	3 years AY	1, 2, 3, 4
Federal work-study payroll records	3 years AY	1, 2, 3, 4
Ledgers identifying SFA transactions	3 years AY	1, 2, 3, 4
Records of SFA program transactions	3 years AY	1, 2, 3, 4
Records of student accounts	3 years AY	1, 2, 3, 4
Records supporting data on required reports (SFA program reconciliation reports, audit reports and school responses, Pell grant statements of accounts; Accrediting and Licensing agency reports)	3 years AY	1, 2, 3, 4
SFA Recipient Records		
Application data submitted to the Dept. of Education or lender by the school on behalf of the student	3 years AY	1, 2, 3, 4
Data used to establish student's admission, enrollment status, period of enrollment	3 years AY	1, 2, 3, 4
Date and amount of disbursements	3 years AY	1, 2, 3, 4
Documentation of student's eligibility	3 years AY	1, 2, 3, 4
Documentation of student's satisfactory academic progress	3 years AY	1, 2, 3, 4
Documentation of student's program of study and enrolled courses	3 years AY	1, 2, 3, 4
Documentation related to the receipt of aid, such as: amount of grant, loan, FWS award; and calculations used to determine aid amounts	3 years AY	1, 2, 3, 4
Documentation of initial or exit loan counseling	3 years AY	1, 2, 3, 4

* **AY:** from award year
^ end of award year
B of student's last attendance
C of report submission

1 Schools may be required to retain records for longer periods of time if the records are involved in an SFA program review, audit or investigation. If the 3 year retention period expires before the issue is resolved, records must be retained until resolution is achieved.
2 Financial Aid records are normally maintained by financial aid offices. The SFA requirements do not, however, mandate that all records be maintained by financial aid offices. Business offices, Admissions and/or Registrars' offices may be more appropriate custodians of financial aid records.
3 Schools must adhere to the record retention requirements upon their closing, change of ownership, termination or suspension from participation in the SFA programs.
4 In addition to keeping records on federal financial aid, institutions are also responsible for the maintenance of financial aid transcripts for transfer students.

Information and Technical Assistance Resources:
- Department of Education Web site for Financial Aid Professionals: http://www.ifap.ed.gov
- Department of Education Technical Support for Financial Aid Administrators: 800-4-ED-SFAP (800-433-7327)

25

TABLE 9: SCHEDULE H—FEDERAL STUDENT FINANCIAL AID (SFA) RECORD RETENTION REQUIREMENTS

Record Series Title/Description	Retention Period Minimal	Notes
Documentation supporting the school's calculation of its completion/graduation or transfer-out rate	3 years AY	1, 2, 3, 4
Documents used to verify applicant's data	3 years AY	1, 2, 3, 4
Financial aid history for transfer students	3 years AY	1, 2, 3, 4
Reports and forms used for participation in the SFA program	3 years AY	1, 2, 3, 4
Student Aid Report (SAR) or Institutional Student Information Record (ISIR)	3 years AY	1, 2, 3, 4
Requirements for Specific Aid		
Borrowers eligibility records	3 years AY[A,B]	1, 2, 3, 4
Campus-based aid (Perkins loan, SEOG, and Federal Work Study)	3 years AY[A]	1, 2, 3, 4
FFEL and Direct Loans:		1, 2, 3, 4
Fiscal Operations Report (FISAP)	3 years AY[A,C]	1, 2, 3, 4
Pell Grant	3 years AY[A]	1, 2, 3, 4
Perkins repayment records	3 years from date loan assigned, cancelled, or repaid	1, 2, 3, 4
Perkins original promissory notes	Until loan is satisfied or documents are needed to enforce obligation	1, 2, 3, 4
All other records/reports	3 years AY[A,C]	1, 2, 3, 4

* **AY:** from award year
[A] end of award year
[B] of student's last attendance
[C] of report submission

[1] Schools may be required to retain records for longer periods of time if the records are involved in an SFA program review, audit or investigation. If the 3 year retention period expires before the issue is resolved, records must be retained until resolution is achieved.
[2] Financial Aid records are normally maintained by financial aid offices. The SFA requirements do not, however, mandate that all records be maintained by financial aid offices. Business offices, Admissions and/or Registrars' offices may be more appropriate custodians of financial aid records.
[3] Schools must adhere to the record retention requirements upon their closing, change of ownership, termination or suspension from participation in the SFA programs.
[4] In addition to keeping records on federal financial aid, institutions are also responsible for the maintenance of financial aid transcripts for transfer students.

Information and Technical Assistance Resources:
- Department of Education Web site for Financial Aid Professionals: http://www.ifap.ed.gov
- Department of Education Technical Support for Financial Aid Administrators: 800-4-ED-SFAP (800-433-7327)

CHAPTER 4

Methods of Storage

by **Charles Toomajian, Registrar and Associate Dean of the College, Williams College (Williamstown, MA)**

The previous section offers guidelines for establishing retention and disposition schedules for the conventional records maintained in the offices of admissions and the registrar. To reduce the cost of maintaining hardcopy documents and to ensure the preservation of permanent records, institutions must establish records retention plans that include storage and backup. The four principal media currently used to store records are paper, micrographics, computer machine-readable media and document management systems, up to and including enterprise content management systems. The major advantages and disadvantages of each storage medium are covered below.

The improvements in this area continue at a rapid pace so the reader should always check with colleagues, both on- and off-campus, when planning a new or different method of storing records. There may well be significant cost savings of one method, or vendor, over others if another office, *e.g.*, the controller's office, already has a working system that you can also use. If your campus becomes involved in an enterprise content management system, of course, all participants will be using the same system.

Paper

Paper, or hard copy, is especially practical when files are small, purged often, and ac-

27

cessed infrequently. The shortcomings of paper storage are timeliness, destructibility, file integrity, and space consumption. Paper takes up more room than any other medium and, because not all paper records are of uniform size, filing them can be troublesome and lead to their being bent or torn. Permanent records kept in paper form should be stored in fireproof file cabinets or vaults and should have a backup on another medium, in a different location, for security. Confidential records should be stored in a file room or file cabinets that can be locked.

Micrographics

Micrographics include computer output microfilm (COM) and source document microfilm. Source document microfilm has long been used as a backup for paper documents whereas COM is an alternative to paper. Traditionally, microfilm has been, and continues to be, used primarily for longterm preservation of records. Advanced micrographics equipment, combined with technology to link those devices to computers, changed that situation toward the end of the last century. At that time, microfilm became a medium more widely used for storing and retrieving numerous active records. Information copied from textual or magnetic media was produced in the form of microfilm or microfiche. Compared to paper, micrographics storage offered considerable savings in costs, space and handling.

COM is a system that produces computer output on microfilm or microfiche. The COM device produces an image of each page of a report or record on microfilm or microfiche.

Source document microfilm consists of hard copy documents photographed on to film. Equipment can be purchased to film records in-house, or the service can be purchased from a vendor. Both COM and source document microfilm can be read by selecting microfilm reels or microfiche cards, and mounting them in a reading device, or using a computerassisted retrieval system (CAR) that automatically locates and mounts the desired frames.

Today microfilm continues to be used widely as a backup medium for records but COM has been replaced by other media in nearly all cases.

A word to the wise—there are a variety of microfilms available and each has different qualities of clarity and resistance to deterioration over time. Therefore it is vital to insure that you choose the film applicable to your needs. "Read the fine print" and "buyer beware" are good approaches when dealing with vendors or sales representatives in general and in this case in particular.

Computer Machine-Readable Records

All colleges and universities use computers to process some student records and most are totally dependent on computer systems to produce course registrations, grade reports, transcripts, and other vital records. When computers are used for data processing, they create computer machine-readable records that may be stored on magnetic media, *e.g.* disks and tapes.

In the past, records managers were mostly concerned with the retention and disposal of records stored on paper and microfilm. Today records managers also must work with the records custodians, the data processing staff, the institutional research office and the archivist to develop policies that govern access, maintenance, retention, disposal and security of machine-readable records.

POLICIES AND PROCEDURES

Policies for the administration and management of machine-readable records should be developed in conjunction with the design of each automated system. Planning for the management of each system should include the following components:

- Policies governing access to the system. Criteria that define authorized access to student records should include computer machine-readable records. Authorized users should be assigned passwords that must be changed frequently. All authorized users should be informed of rules and regulations that govern disclosure of information and alteration of records.
- Procedures to keep track of all access to the system and all changes made to records in the system (audit trails). Each system should be monitored regularly for unauthorized access or alteration of records.
- Proper retention and disposal of data. Decisions regarding the proper retention of data must take into account the need to access or update the records at some future date. Procedures should be designed to remove inactive records from active files and databases by deleting information no longer needed. Data that may be needed in the future should be transferred to magnetic tape, microfilm, or paper.
- Maintenance of the computer hardware and software necessary to access the records. The hardware and software required to access machine-readable records must be maintained as long as the records remain active. When a computer system is replaced with a new system or when new programs are designed to process records, all existing machine-readable records, including inactive records in storage, should be converted to a format compatible with the new system.
- Measures to avoid inadvertent loss of information caused by human error, machine malfunction, or natural disaster. A duplicate copy of all valuable records stored on disks or tapes should be stored in a secure, offsite location. Backup copies should be kept uptodate so they can be used to recreate any records that might be lost accidentally. Essential documentation needed to operate the system and interpret information in machine-readable records should be produced in duplicate. One copy of the documentation should be stored off site.

Policies and procedures for the management of machine-readable records should be established when a system is designed rather than waiting until it has been in operation for some time. However, policies for the access, security, management and retention of data should be developed and applied retroactively, if necessary, to all systems currently in place. In addition, policies should be reviewed often and changed as appropriate.

Institutions may need access to machine-readable records for extended periods of time. The longterm storage of machine-readable records requires a carefully controlled storage environment and regular maintenance procedures. Records managers should work with the dataprocessing staff to ensure that machine-readable records are stored under conditions that will increase their longevity.

Some machine-readable records may have longterm value for statistical analysis and other research purposes. Records that contain data on the demographic characteristics of students, course offerings, enrollment, financial aid, and student performance may be of particular interest to social scientists, educators, and historians. Some college and university archives acquire and preserve machine-readable records, and many campuses have social science data libraries that preserve data in machine-readable form.

The institution's archivist and institutional researcher, who may be interested in preserving them or may recommend an appropriate repository, should be contacted before disposal of machine-readable records with possible longterm research value.

Document Management Systems

A document management system, or DMS, is a computer system for tracking and storing electronic documents and/or images of paper documents. It may be used by a single office or selected multiple offices.

The latest approach to overall document management is an expansion of DMS to enterprise content management, or ECM, which is the software, technologies, tools and methods used to capture, manage, store, preserve and deliver electronic content across an enterprise. It includes document scanning, intelligent data capture, workflow, records management, electronic document management (EDM), computer output to laser disk (COLD)/enterprise report management (ERM), collaboration and e-mail message archive and e-mail retrieval. To be most effective, as the name suggests, the system should include all offices within the institution, or "enterprise," that deal with student and alumni records.

BENEFITS OF DMS/ECM SYSTEMS

- **Improved Access:** Documents are stored online and therefore are immediately and easily available to all authorized to view them. With ECM, inter-office requests to search and retrieve paper versions of these documents can be eliminated. In addition, an imaging system allows multiple people to view a given document simultaneously, thereby reducing the need to pass paper documents from one person to the next (and risk their loss).

- **Time Savings:** Making documents available online decreases the time needed for various tasks by eliminating the circulation of physical documents. Specifically for admissions and the registrar, processes that benefit include the reading of admission applications by multiple readers and the transfer of student records and related documents from admissions to the registrar.

- **Document Preservation:** Once scanned and added to the system repository, documents can be backed up automatically.
- **Reduction of Consumables:** Reducing the need for paper, paper recycling, printers, toner cartridges, and printer maintenance reduces both costs and labor as offices move to online content management. Once fully implemented, content management systems significantly reduce the need to print documents.
- **Space Savings:** As mentioned earlier, no medium takes up as much space as paper, and an effective ECM system virtually eliminates the need for keeping paper documents. Developing ECM capabilities is likely to be more cost-effective than finding additional space for paper files.
- **Modest Monetary Savings:** There is no need to microfilm paper records for backup and/or storage. In admissions, there is no need for folders. Over several years, the savings can be substantial.

It is important to note that some states have provisions on the medium in which the record is retained. For example, Texas allows electronic retention of records, whether created electronically or transferred from a paper format. New Jersey, on the other hand, has state provisions that do not recognize document imaging at face value, but instead regard microfilm as the primary storage method, only approving document imaging systems on a case-by-case basis. Due to the varying conditions among different states, it is essential to review your state's provisions before deciding on a particular medium of storage.

PROBLEMS AND ISSUES

The implementation of a document management system, whether for a single office, selected multiple offices or the whole institution, requires more preliminary work than is often realized. It is imperative to ascertain what is required of the system before selecting it, a process that must include all participants whose needs may vary substantially. It is also important to keep the assessment process moving and not allow the participants to get bogged down.

A successful system implementation requires involving all stakeholders as much as possible from the beginning. What seems reasonable to the IT experts may not seem so to the department heads. It is also important to involve the staff who will be using the system regularly; because of their intimate knowledge of how things are done now, these front-line folks often anticipate problems that others do not. Remember that an existing "bad" system of record management will not become a "good" system simply by moving toward ECM. It is even likely that weaknesses will become more pronounced as more than one office becomes involved and components such as workflow are introduced. Work the kinks out early in the process!

In spite of what vendors say, there isn't a worthwhile system that works "out of the box." Be prepared, and allot enough time and resources to the implementation phase. Even though not inexpensive, it is often cost-effective to outsource some of the implementation. Be sure to save some of the budget for this phase!

Don't underestimate the impact of the change upon staff. With ECM, it is impossible to hide from others. The advantages of an institution-wide approach to records management bring with them a new distribution of work. Many people's jobs are likely to change. Some will have more work, while others will have less. Some people will feel liberated by not having to deal with paper while others will feel lost. Leadership will be needed to address the inevitable individual gains and losses and keep people focused on the improvements.

POLICIES AND PROCEDURES

Of course, as with all records storage, policies and procedures must be in place to assure the integrity of the records.

- A firmly established and maintained security system must be in place. Most systems offer as much security as any user needs. Passwords are a must, and value-based security is needed in a network environment. Security systems that mimic student information systems are required in a shared environment.
- Firm rules of retention and disposal should be followed. With any electronic storage medium, it is far too easy to keep everything. Eventually, this approach will cause storage and retrieval problems.
- Users should be planning for the future as soon as they begin to consider using this technology. It is imperative to have a system with architecture that stores images in standard format. The technology will continue to change, so it is necessary that the stored information be transportable to future systems.

STORAGE AND MAINTENANCE

Document imaging is the most efficient method of storing data. Any new records storage plans should seriously address document imaging as the storage method of choice. This technology is aligned with the already accepted student information systems. Further, it can make the combination of the two seamless, by, for instance, using the database in the student information system as the database for the scanned images.

Document imaging, then, is simply one more method of storing records. It is the answer to many storage problems as are the other options. Each institution obviously has to make its own choice. However, there must be a storage plan with a back up option at all institutions. And it is the responsibility of the record keepers to make sure such policies and practices are in place.

CHAPTER 5

Security of Student Records

by **Susan Van Voorhis, Director of Academic Support Resources and University Registrar, University of Minnesota – Twin Cities (Minneapolis, MN)**

As a records retention plan is implemented, it is important to ensure the security of student records. While this chapter will focus primarily on records stored using electronic technologies, the security of paper records will also be addressed. Student records systems should provide timely and efficient access to, and retrieval of, student records data. These systems should also include and apply security controls for access to ensure the integrity of records is not easily compromised or access given to staff who do not need it. In addition, vital records must receive top security priority in any program or system. A skillfully devised and carefully monitored records retention and maintenance program will aid in identifying such records and in providing for their security.

Records managers must take appropriate management measures to reduce vulnerability of records to loss and alteration through human error, natural disaster, deterioration, sabotage, accident, negligence, fraud, system conversion, technological "disaster," or technological obsolescence. Trends and developments in communications, recordkeeping techniques and technology have all contributed to an increase in the vulnerability of student records to loss and alteration. Moreover, the complexity of records management and the difficulty associated with maintaining effective security programs have grown with

33

the increased use of data communications, integrated databases, networks, and sophisticated processing techniques. The trend toward decentralization of data and systems has created new security concerns and educating all involved parties who use student data is imperative to protecting it.

Maintaining data integrity for computerized systems must take into account data entry errors, programming errors, and accidental as well as unauthorized changes of files. Security can be improved through the use of passwords, a log of updates, audits and periodic audit reports showing changes made in the files.

Records managers must continue to reduce the cost of records maintenance; however, they must retain records as required by federal, state, and other regulatory agencies and be able to retrieve documents or data as required, including easy access to archived information.

Technology and System Planning

As technology continues to change, security programs designed to protect student records data must be sustained. This can be costly and time consuming, so it is important to evaluate the cost and the return on investment. The following is a list of some items to consider when evaluating the appropriateness of a security plan for a student records system:

- Prevention of potential security breaches
- Identity management capabilities
- Potential to upgrade as technology changes
- Protection of records against loss in all media types

- Ability to ensure appropriate security measures and standards are implemented and enforced
- Ability to detect potential issues such as system breaches, system backup issues or server problems before they become a crisis
- Limiting the extent of loss of data if a crisis occurs (determine backup schedule)
- Prevention and monitoring of unauthorized access
- Providing for audit and control on a continuing basis
- Ensuring data protection at a reasonable cost
- Ease of administration and making necessary changes
- Facilitation of the normal working tasks of the institution.

The scope of a records security program will vary with the size and complexity of the system it is designed to protect. Since this undertaking usually involves considerable cost, professional assistance should be sought to assess the adequacy of a program.

Planning security for any system should include the following ten phases:

PHASE 1: PREPARE FOR SECURE STUDENT RECORDS SYSTEMS.

- List potential risks, such as fire, earthquake, lightning, water, radiation, extreme temperature changes, sabotage, theft, explosion, machine malfunction, machine damage, erasure, transmission error, write-over (grade change), mismarking, vermin, misplacing information or documents, power outages, media deterioration and losses due to hardware and software conversions.

- Investigate implementation of an identity management system and its impact on other systems.
- Review safeguards that limit access to restricted areas (server rooms), functions, and systems.
- Determine security procedures for, and frequency of, checking equipment, networks, and facilities.
- Establish a plan for maintaining the data integrity of online systems.
- Prepare a disaster recovery plan for the office working with the information technology.
- Ensure "dependency" areas (*e.g.*, information technology) have a continuity/recovery plan. Store a copy in an offcampus location.

PHASE 2: EVALUATE OR ESTABLISH SAFEGUARDS FOR SYSTEMS.

- Ensure that sufficient documentation exists so that data and programs could be reconstructed if necessary.
- Review security procedures at both primary and backup sites to ensure against fraud or loss through accidental or willful destruction.
- Conduct student records orientation sessions or create tutorials covering FERPA and institutional privacy policies. Record attendance of each authorized user.
- Determine procedures for employee termination and provide for the recovery of keys, badges, and restricted access to information and materials. Passwords, lock combinations, and intrusion alarm codes should be changed each time an employee with access leaves employment.

- Create a process to analyze and adjust the security access for staff transferring to another unit within the institution.
- Inspect safeguards utilized in all processes of operations control, personnel supervision, and recordkeeping, as well as data and output handling, to ensure the accuracy and completeness of data and the detection and correction of errors.
- Identify and arrange for alternate processing facilities to be made available in the event of an extended loss of computer facilities. (This is dependent on the information technology unit's continuity plan.)
- Evaluate computer system controls from the standpoint of both data processing and the user access. For example, data handling procedures institution-wide described in detail, program standards documented, and testing techniques defined to assist staff performing functions that impact data.
- Review and establish increased security procedures relative to password access to Internet, wireless, or remote access.
- Examine insurance for scope of coverage, particularly in regard to exclusions and compliance requirements written into the policies.

PHASE 3: DEVELOP A WRITTEN PLAN THAT ADDRESSES THE IDENTIFIED CONCERNS.

- Address issues and concerns in the plan, distribute for stakeholder review and sign off on agreement.

- Charge someone with reviewing the plan on an annual basis. The responsible party should bring forward any changes or identified issues and follow up to ensure compliance.
- Work with other departments and units to ensure concerns are addressed and documents are updated.
- Update information and confirm agreement of procedures with relevant units.

PHASE 4: ASSIGN PRIORITIES FOR IMPLEMENTATION.

When implementing security for a student records system, it is imperative that the scope is defined and priorities are set before implementation begins. This will minimize future problems and address many potential issues in advance. The records manager must work with the information technology unit to ensure the appropriate security will be in place. All parties must understand what will be implemented and where there might be potential security issues.

PHASE 5: IMPLEMENT A PLAN OR CREATE A POLICY DEFINING ROLES AND RESPONSIBILITIES IN REGARDS TO MAINTAINING THE SECURITY OF STUDENT RECORDS. ENSURE THAT ALL STAFF PARTICIPATE IN AN AWARENESS PROGRAM.

Establish a clear and concise policy regarding responsibilities. Doing so will allow for better training and a solid understanding of staff roles and expectations. Clear expectations and pre-established consequences will also make it easier to handle any policy breaches

by staff, if they should occur. Refresher training should occur on a regular basis.

PHASE 6: APPOINT SPECIFIC INDIVIDUALS AND A BACKUP TO ASSUME RESPONSIBILITY FOR THE ENFORCEMENT AND CONTROL OF EACH PROCEDURE.

Responsible parties are to regularly review, update, and communicate any procedure changes to the relevant areas. The staff or unit with security responsibilities needs to ensure procedures are followed and rules are enforced. If there is a breach, data managers should be informed, a review conducted, and appropriate measures taken to ensure the incident does not recur.

PHASE 7: PROVIDE COMPREHENSIVE REVIEW FOR COMPLIANCE AND EFFECTIVENESS OF SYSTEM SECURITY.

It is important to conduct a review of various systems to ensure they are secure. Also, a review of those staff with access to multiple system components should be conducted annually to ensure that broad access is still required for their tasks and their access meets auditor approval. Separation of duties should be outlined in the roles and responsibilities policy to assist with this process.

PHASE 8: ESTABLISH AN INTERNAL AUDIT TO ENSURE DATA TAMPERING DOES NOT EXIST. LIMIT ACCESS AND ESTABLISH SEPARATION OF DUTIES TO ENSURE SECURITY CONFIDENCE.

In most student information systems, there is a vast amount of data available to view and

36

update. It is imperative that there is an audit trail of what transactions have occurred and by which staff or student employee. An audit trail should be documented either within a system or via a report. Employees and student staff with access to update student records and also with an academic record at the institution should have their student records audited on at least a random basis. Ideally the staff creating the initial student admissions record should not also have the ability to register students for courses and insert final grades. However, since this is often not possible at smaller institutions, thoughtful training and regular monitoring should take place to help minimize the opportunity for data tampering. Documentation should outline disciplinary actions that will be taken if data policies are violated.

PHASE 9: CREATE A COMPREHENSIVE COMMUNICATION PLAN THAT INCLUDES NEW EMPLOYEE ROLES AND RESPONSIBILITIES, YEARLY REMINDER INFORMATION, AND POLICY REVIEWS.

Communication is the key to keeping the institution's employees updated on various changes to policies and procedures. Staff is expected to keep up on the latest information on data security. However, because there is so much information to which staff must be attuned, institutions should ensure they are communicating information that directly impacts their situation.

PHASE 10: DEVELOP PROCESSES TO INVESTIGATE PROBLEMS AND ALLEGED VIOLATIONS OF POLICIES. REFER VIOLATIONS TO APPROPRIATE OFFICES FOR RESOLUTION OR DISCIPLINARY ACTION.

While it is difficult for managers to believe that an employee may violate data policies, a process for investigating alleged violations and guidelines for consequences needs to be established. When violations to the data policy have been substantiated, managers should follow the documented disciplinary procedures.

Other Considerations

Investigate consolidating security administration within one central organization. This unit would make recommendations on needed changes in organizational structure. This unit should work with data managers or data custodians to define and implement a consistent approach for security administration applied across all platforms and systems.

There are effective access and security programs or setups available if appropriate for many systems. Ensure records are not subject to unauthorized use and cannot be altered or destroyed. Staff with a need to know must have access to records, so facilitate this wherever possible.

When it comes to systems or technical staff, consider whether they need access to both test and production data. This could be a potential security issue. Technical staff with production access with no oversight may manipulate student records. It is also possible that a developer is mistakenly working in production instead of the test system, which could damage the integrity of student records. One option to improve security is to grant production access to on-call staff members only during the time they are on call. This process could vary at each institution.

Ensure access requests are properly completed and authorized, and all required training courses or tutorials are completed. The entire process should be outlined in a procedures document.

TYPES OF ACCESS TO SYSTEMS, NETWORKS AND DATA:

- **Authentication** is the process of entering a password to access information. The password identifies the person or party accessing the system. Once a staff member authenticates, access to information should relate only to the tasks they need to accomplish.
- **Two-factor authentication** is a security process in which the user provides two means of identification. One is typically a physical token, such as a card, and the other is typically something memorized, such as a security code. In this context, the two factors involved are sometimes spoken of as *something you have* and *something you know*.
- **Data warehouse, web services, and business intelligence** allow for reporting to occur with accurate information at a centralized or decentralized level; access and guidelines need to be established for determining who and how someone gains access to this information. Databases must have strong security measures in place to minimize potential hacking.

- **Identity management systems** allow for the combination of business process and technology used to manage data on IT systems and applications about users. Managed data includes user objects, identity attributes, security privileges and authentication factors. These systems can eliminate some security concerns; however, it is important that data managers, data custodians and information technology staff all be involved in the implementation and ongoing support of this type of system.

SECURITY OF PAPER RECORDS

Many units have gone paperless; however, in some cases paper documents are still used for various functions. Transcripts, certification and verification letters, and diplomas can be in a paper format and need to be secure and protected. Some of these documents contain confidential information and therefore need to be treated with the same protection principles as any other private data.

One of the data protection principles is that records must be kept secure. In terms of paper records, this means that you must:

- Ensure office area is secure;
- Make sure your paper filing system is locked;
- Use confidential recycling or a secure shredding system to dispose of paper records;
- Secure confidential documents and do not leave in the open;
- Ensure only those staff who need to use the data have access to it;

- Remind staff about importance of security of student records;
- Establish a plan to avoid deterioration of records like paper, microfilm, or microfiche (see Chapter 4, Methods of Storage), and
- Have processes in place to secure the vast amount of paper records handled in an imaging area.

Recommendations for Staff

- Check employment screening practices for persons holding positions that require the handling of confidential information.
- Staff should complete an annual compliance statement that indicates awareness of the repercussions for violating access policy.
- Staff should lock their computer when stepping away from a workstation.
- Password strength should follow recommended guidelines.
- Passwords should never be shared with other staff.
- Assign a staff member to stay current on federal and state guidelines.

Summary

In many institutions, official student records are now only in electronic formats due to systems such as imaging which allow an office to become paperless. However, the security of unofficial paper student records will continue to be a concern as many staff still print paper records or screen shots and do not recycle confidential materials appropriately. Staff may unintentionally leave confidential documents out in the open, so offices must be secure. Reminders to staff about confidential document security are important. Also, as systems continue to allow for more data to be available in multiple media, data managers must continue to update, monitor, and audit the security on systems and make changes as appropiate.

In summary, data security policies and procedures should be:
- Simple to use;
- Secure and confidential;
- Accurate, reliable and consistent;
- Cost effective and easy to maintain;
- Expandable and adaptable to meet future needs, and
- Designed so that it's easy to retrieve relevant information.

CHAPTER 6

Policy Development for Academic Departments

Grand Valley State University Case Study

by **Jerry Montag, University Registrar, Grand Valley State University**
and **Pat Smith, Deputy University Counsel, Grand Valley State University**

For many years, registrars wondered why other department offices insisted on storing documents that were already filed either electronically, on paper or were microfilmed/microfiched in the registrar's offices. Registrars were painfully aware that duplicate copies of items were routinely being kept by a number of offices on campus such as change of grade forms, declaration of majors, and the "third copy" of a four part NCR form which, although unreadable, listed the student' requested courses for registration.

If you asked departments why they kept these types of forms, the typical answer would be that they wanted to have backup copies as needed, or that it was simply easier to locate the document in the department office as opposed to the registrar's office. Over time, the retention of these documents became a challenge since space is always at a premium (especially in a faculty member's office) and the piles of records maintained became overwhelming.

41

The registrar's office was asked to develop a policy that clearly laid out the items that departments should keep, for how long, where to file them, when to purge them, etc. In my initial enthusiasm, I envisioned an all-encompassing policy that addressed a myriad of documents such as travel receipts, faculty research papers, résumés, awards received, grants expenditures and a million other items (or so it seemed). After clarification, I was told to focus on items maintained only in academic department offices.

Not having a guidebook to tell me how to get my arms around this project even in its simplified form, I initially began to formulate the process and procedure by reading *AACRAO's Retention of Records* guide, and many articles and data on the Web. With the wealth of information on the topic, it became clear that I needed to focus on the AACRAO guidelines for campuses and what academic departments retained at my institution.

Where do you begin?

The first step was to ask my colleague from the Office of the University Counsel to join me as co-chair of the group of academic/administrative personnel. I had originally envisioned a large committee that would meet on a regular basis but instead appealed to a select group of academic advisors or department administrators. The committee members knew how their staff had maintained the filing system for department heads and deans, and had varied approaches as to what they kept for how long and why. The group was open-minded to the possibility of change.

A simple alternative or additional method of gaining awareness as to academic department records practices is to send a survey to registrar's offices around the country. The survey I asked colleagues to complete was limited to institutions with similar characteristics since the philosophy of what to keep may be the same due to governance, state/private control, board requirements, etc.

Why implement a records retention policy for academic departments?

Though some members of the committee were initially unconvinced a policy was necessary, it took only a few meetings for reality to sink in. Important questions arose such as:

- Why are items duplicated and the copies retained in several different offices on campus?
- Is there storage space on campus?
- Why are there varying opinions about how long to keep a document?
- Is there a uniform policy, and if so, is anyone adhering to it? If not, what might such a policy address and resolve?

It was discovered that many departments already had a "shadow" records retention system in place they had come up with on their own. One college realized that no university guidelines for academic departments had been established, so they developed their own policy and filing standards.

Other departments either kept everything or sundry items. Some of the departments were mindful of retention schedules dictated by accreditation guidelines and were under the impression that the accrediting agency required them to keep the original documents. However, the agency clarified that a copy of a document kept and produced upon request would suffice as original and official for their purposes.

Challenges Faced by the Committee

Change is always a challenge since it involves letting go of a standard process or procedure. Some members were initially uncomfortable with the registrar's office serving as a central filing center instead of keeping copies within their own departments. In addition, a number of people didn't realize the breadth of documents kept by the registrar's office. At Grand Valley State, all types of academic records are immediately scanned in the Office of the Records and Registration (including all types of admissions documents).

What should an academic records retention policy address?

The guidelines the committee used were simple—it followed both AACRAO and state guidelines. Each institution must identify the means and ends of a campus policy and what is appropriate for the institution.

The Politics Involved

Reality dictates that you will never please everybody. People don't want to get rid of, for instance, faculty evaluations because they are afraid that students or faculty would appeal something from years before. The committee did not dictate that departments not keep

duplicate copies but instead explained that they could access the documents elsewhere on campus.

FERPA

FERPA laws do not encompass handwritten notes stuffed into a faculty member's drawer or inside a file folder in a faculty member's department. FERPA also does not apply to personal notes kept by a faculty or staff member that do not become part of the student's educational record. However, FERPA protects notes kept in the registrar's office as part of the official record of the student. The committee encouraged faculty members to destroy or purge their personal file notes, warning that the notes may come back later to haunt them.

Statute of Limitations

It is appropriate for departments to dispose of records because most laws provide time limits for an appeal of situations such as grade complaints, contractual agreements, or the reasons behind acceptance or rejection of tenure for a faculty member. Of course, campuses must know whether this time limit is within the policy requirements of the state in which the institution resides, the legal policy of the institution and the institution's "level of comfort." Simply stated, if your institution's academic offices would rather keep something longer than required by law, it certainly may do so. The State of Michigan mandates six years on the statute of limitations for contracts. However, the policy developed by the Grand Valley State committee uses a seven-

TABLE 10: RECOMMENDED ACADEMIC DEPARTMENT OFFICES RECORDS RETENTION AND DISPOSAL POLICY*

Items to Be Retained	Description	Length[1]	By Whom
Academic Records	Copy of student's courses, credits, grades, scores on proficiency/placement examinations, education and enrollment verifications, transcript requests, copies of i-20's and other pertinent data representing their academic history at your institution	P	Registrar
Advising Plans	Notes from faculty after advisement sessions with students	5 yrs[2]	Department
Appeal for Change of Grade	Student requested through their department a review and consideration of a different final grade	1 yr	Department
Appeals to Registrar	Examples of appeals may include time limits for graduation, residency, tuition refund, retroactive withdrawals, tuition appeals, etc.	P	Registrar
Applications for Admission	Applicants who *do not* enroll, whether they are accepted or rejected	P	Registrar
		1 yr[3]	Department[4]
	Applicants who enroll	P	Registrar
		5 yrs[2]	Department[4]
Applications for Graduation	Form a student completes and submits to the registrar's office informing them of their intent to graduate at the end of the specified semester	P	Registrar
Blackboard Accounts	Instructor virtual grade book	1 yr[5]	Information Technology
Catalog Information	Data submitted to be included in catalog from academic departments	P	Registrar
Class Lists	Roster of students enrolled in class at time of printing list	P[6]	Registrar
Correspondence	To and from faculty member regarding student issues	5 yrs[2]	Department
Course Syllabi	Instructor outline of the course requirements. May include information about tests, projects, reading assignments, as well as required textbooks	5 yrs[7]	Department
Courses Offered Per Semester	Schedule of classes	P	Registrar
Declaration of Majors	Form a student completes to declare/change a major	P	Registrar
Department Files for Secondary Admits	Additional information departments may keep on these types of programs	5 yrs[8]	Department
Disciplinary Actions on Students	Information received	5 yrs[2]	Department[11]
Examinations, Tests, Quizzes	Examinations, tests, quizzes, and term papers used to demonstrate student's knowledge of materials learned in a particular course	1 yr	Department

* The information in this document is based on the recommended time period outlined in the retention of records manual by the American Association of Collegiate Registrars and Admissions Officers (AACRAO), 2000

[1] **P**: Permanent
[2] from date of graduation or last date of eligibility for UG (Undergraduate) and GR (Graduate) students within their degree program time limits
[3] after application term
[4] optional; some departments keep additional required information on students
[5] archived after retention period
[6] no need to keep pre-Banner copies
[7] from date last offered by department unless accreditation board requires a different retention period
[8] from date of graduation or last date of attendance
[9] determined by program or accreditation
[10] archived in bound or digital format
[11] or appropriate administrative office in the case of non-academic records

TABLE 10: RECOMMENDED ACADEMIC DEPARTMENT OFFICES RECORDS RETENTION AND DISPOSAL POLICY*

Items to Be Retained	Description	Length[1]	By Whom
Examinations for Credit or Placement	Scores from tests and your institution equivalencies for AP, CLEP and other types of standardized tests	P	Registrar
Exceptions to Repeat Policies	Students who complete a form to request an exception to the existing repeat course policy	P	Registrar
Faculty Course Evaluations	Forms completed by students evaluating various aspects of the teaching of courses	7 yrs	Department
Grade Changes	Forms faculty submitted to change a grade for a student in a particular course and semester	P	Registrar
Grades Received by Students	List of the mid term and final grades submitted by the faculty for students in their class for the semester	P	Registrar
Graduation Audits	Evaluation of registrar's office staff to determine if a student met all the requirements to be awarded their degree	P	Registrar
Health Related Programs Health Forms	Copies of physical examinations, immunizations and other documents		Department[9]
Master's or Doctoral Students	Thesis or final project report, or (in health related programs) protocol	P	Library[10]
Permit Overrides for Classes	Approvals for students to register for classes that have certain restrictions	P	Registrar
Registration and Drop/Add	Forms students may complete when registering for classes or making changes to their schedule	P	Registrar
Schedule of Classes forms	Used by department for submission to record's office during the schedule development cycle	1 yr	Department
Transfer Credit	Your institution-approved transfer credit equivalencies and copies of transcripts from other colleges and universities	P	Registrar
Waiver/Substitutions	Department approval of courses requested for degree requirements	P	Registrar

DEVELOPING A PROCESS FOR THE PURGING OF RECORDS

Purging is a process of removing all unwanted, unneeded or useless data that may be maintained in a file that has lost its value. As noted in the recommended records retention and disposal policy, certain documents should be maintained for a limited number of years.

Example: A department is keeping a master file of all correspondence received by the faculty member from the student in an alphabetical order and will keep the data for five years. There are two ways to keep this data—either by alpha order or by a yearly order.

If alpha order, the department will need to review and purge those documents in the file at the end of every year to weed out those files that are no longer needed (have exceeded the five year requirement). If by yearly order, the department will need to purge the data that is more than five years old. In either scenario, if the unnecessary data is not periodically purged, the volume of data becomes unmanageable.

OVERALL RECOMMENDATIONS

- Departments are advised when shredding large numbers of documents to use a company recommended by university. Please contact your purchasing office for additional information.
- Departments need to develop a policy and process to periodically purge documents—see above for additional detailed information on this process.
- *Maintained permanently by the registrar* indicates the item is scanned into the student's file or data is stored in Banner. There is no need to keep another copy in the department.
- *Five years* means from date of graduation or last date of eligibility for UG and GR students within their degree program time limits
- If a document is to be kept for 1 year or less, do not scan the document in the interim. Keep and then shred after 1 year.

year retention schedule to ensure that nothing is tossed out prematurely.

Important Note: If there are files on students, faculty or staff that are part of ongoing litigation or potential lawsuits, retain it all. You may need to refer to the original documents as your legal counsel proceeds.

Shred or Keep?

Departments must realize that faculty office space and department space are always a premium. The simplest way is to scan everything and shred after scanning, preferably using a reliable outside company.

Give Departments a Choice

The divisions we worked with were very appreciative of the efforts the committee took to develop a department-friendly policy. Our committee suggested that departments may choose to retain documents longer than delineated in the policy.

Process Summary

- Review other university policies
- Develop a policy that ensures adequate length of time for retention of records and process for destruction of obsolete records
- Work towards eliminating the retention of duplicate data in two different places/offices
- Scan everything
- Continuously review policy document to ensure its ongoing applicability to issues that arise on campus.

The "Recommended Academic Department Offices Records Retention and Disposal Policy" of Grand Valley State University is provided in Table 10, on page 44.

APPENDIX **A**

Sample Records Inventory Form

Name or Title of Record _____

Inclusive Dates of Record _____

Summary of Record Content _____

Office _____

Record Storage _____

Frequency of Record Reference:

    How often is record initiated?   ○ Daily ○ Weekly ○ Monthly ○ Quarterly ○ Annually ○ Other

    How often is record updated?   ○ Daily ○ Weekly ○ Monthly ○ Quarterly ○ Annually ○ Other

    How often is record used?   ○ Daily ○ Weekly ○ Monthly ○ Quarterly ○ Annually ○ Other

    Are records still created?   ○ Yes ○ No

Record Volume:

    Annual accumulation _____ linear ft. OR _____ cubic ft.

    Total accumulation ____ linear ft. OR _____ cubic ft.

Filing Method: ○ Alphabetic ○ Numeric ○ Other_____

Record Medium: ○ Document ○ Email ○ Scan ○ Magnetic Tape ○ Microfilm ○ Other

If record has copies, indicate distribution for the following:

Copy	Color	Office Sent To
Original		
2nd		
3rd		
4th		
5th		
6th		

Recommended Retention Period:

    In Operating Area _____ In Storage Area _____

Justification _____

Disposal Method _____

Inventory Taken By_____ Date _____

Offices _____ Phone _____

Name of Official Custodian_____ Date _____

Office _____ Phone _____

Sample Institutional Records Policy

The records and information management committee governs the retention, safety and disposal of all student records in order to be certain that the information collected, stored, and disseminated is consistent with state and federal guidelines.

The records and information management committee or data custodian is charged with monitoring all systems which contain personally identifiable information in order that each individual's right to privacy is protected, that the information collected is used only for the purpose for which it was intended, and that every safeguard to protect that privacy has been made by each office which has access to such information. The records and information management committee is further charged to:

- Develop a set of appraisal standards to determine the academic, administrative, fiscal, legal, and historical/research value of each student record in compliance with state and federal regulations;

- Ensure that data, records and documents deemed by the committee to have value are adequately protected and maintained;

- Assist the archivist in the development of retention standards for records which have archival value; develop a records and data management program for all vital records;

- Publish a retention and disposal schedule that is in compliance with local, state, and federal laws. Before publication and implementation of this schedule, legal review and official institutional sanction should be secured;

- Designate a member or members of the committee to monitor legislative impact on record retention, data and recordkeeping practices; review periodically the policies created;
- Create a communication plan to inform the institutional community of state and federal guidelines;
- Develop a training program or tutorial for institutional personnel responsible for the storage and maintenance of records;
- Insist that all offices within the institution adhere to the published record retention and disposal schedule; assist offices within the institution in improving their records control and security systems;
- Assist in the development of guidelines for due process to correct any violation of fair information practices.

Membership of the records committee shall include the registrar or designate the records manager, the director of financial aid, the director of admissions, the comptroller, the director of the computer center, human resources designee, data custodian, and the director of institutional research. The chairperson is the vice president for academic affairs, and the archivist serves as the executive secretary.

Pertinent Federal Regulations References

Federal Aid Regulations

Federal Family Education Loan (FFEL)	34 CFR 682
Federal Direct Stafford Loan	34 CFR 682
William D. Ford Federal Direct Loan	34 CFR 685
Pell Grant Program	34 CFR 690
Perkins Loan Program	34 CFR 674
Federal Work Study Program	34 CFR 675
Supplemental Educational Opportunity Grant	34 CFR 676
Higher Education Opportunity Act	PL 110-315
Health Professions and Nursing Student Loans Programs	42 CFR 57.215, 42 CFR 57.315
Veterans Education and Training Benefits	38 CFR 21.42009
Internal Revenue Service Institutional Tax Exemptions	26 CFR 301.201, 26 CFR 702
Agency for International Development (AID)	22 CFR 215, 22 CFR 218

Federal Disclosure and Reporting Regulations

Fair and Accurate Credit Transactions Act 2003 (Red Flag Rules for Identifying and Mitigating Identity Theft)	PL 108-159
Family Educational Rights and Privacy Act (FERPA)	34 CFR 99
Gramm-Leach-Bliley Act (Financial Services Modernization Act)	15 USCS § 6801-6809, et seq. 106, PL 102, 113 Stat. 1338
FTC Data Safeguarding Rule	16 CFR 314
FTC Privacy Rule	16 CFR 313
Student Right-to-Know and Campus Security Act of 1990 (Campus Security Act changed to Jeanne Clery Disclosure Act in the 1998 HEA amendments)	PL 101-542, 34 CFR Part 688.47, 34 CFR Part 688.24
Equity in Athletics Disclosure Act of 1994 Program Participant Agreement	34 CFR 668.14
Solomon Amendment	32 CFR Part 216
Student Assistance General Provisions Act	34 Part 668
Drug Free Workplace Act of 1998	PL 101-690
Drug Free Schools and Communities Act	PL 101-226
Electronic Signatures in Global and National Commerce Act	Public Law 106-229
Taxpayer Relief Act of 1997 (provides for the Hope Scholarships/ Lifetime Learning Tax Credits 26 CFR 1.25A-1)	IRS Notice 97-69, PL 105-34, 111 Stat. 788

* **CFR:** Code of Federal Regulations; **PL:** Public Law

Policies Covering Disposition of Academic Records of Closed Schools

Copies of the Federal Register and the Codes of Federal Regulations are available via the federal National Archives and Records Administration Web site (*www.nara.gov/fedreg/*).

Alabama. Policies are unspecified. Records of one school that closed were taken over by an associated abbey. Records for St. Bernard are at the abbey and the records for Cullman College (formerly Sacred Heart) are at the associated Convent. The Alabama College System (state 2-year colleges and Athens State College junior and senior years only) records for closed schools would be kept by the ACS in Montgomery. No state universities have closed.

Alaska. Records are stored in a central location: Alaska Commission on Postsecondary Education, 3030 Vintage Boulevard, Juneau, AK 99801; (907) 465-2962 or toll-free (800) 441-2962.

Arizona. Current state law specifies that any state college or university that closes must transfer academic records to: State Department of Library Archives and Public Records, Records Management Division, 1919 W Jefferson, Phoenix, AZ 85009; (602) 255-3741. Academic records of private postsecondary schools which close will be retained by: Private Postsecondary Education Board, 1812 W Monroe, Phoenix, AZ 85007; (602) 229-2591.

53

Arkansas. The accrediting agency in the Department of Higher Education assumes responsibility for relocating records: Department of Higher Education, 114 E Capitol Avenue, Little Rock, AR 72201; (501) 371-2000.

California. General information can be found at the California Postsecondary Education Commission (*www.cpec.ca.gov*). The Bureau for Private Postsecondary and Vocational Education became inoperative on July 1, 2007. The Bureau is now closed. The Bureau cannot commence operations unless and until a statute is enacted that creates a new California Private Postsecondary Education Act. Currently, in California, there is no regulatory body with oversight of private postsecondary schools. A temporary solution provides that the Director of the Department of Consumer Affairs could enter into voluntary agreements with institutions operating in California. A list of the custodian of records is available at *www.bppve.ca.gov*. The Web site for the California Department of Consumer Affairs is *www.dca.ca.gov*.

Colorado. For information about closing a public college or university, please contact the Colorado Department of Higher Education (CDHE) (*http://highered.colorado.gov/dhedefault.html*). For information about what to do with records from a private occupational school, please see the following CDHE guide: *http://highered.colorado.gov/DPOS/Schools/closeschool.html*.

Connecticut. Check with the Department of Higher Education, 61 Woodland Street, Hartford, CT 06105; (860) 947-1800.

Delaware. By statute, records are stored at a central location: Delaware Higher Education Commission, Carvel State Office Building, 820 N French Street, Wilmington, DE 19801; (302) 577-3240.

District of Columbia. Check with the Office of Postsecondary Education Research and Assistance, Suite 401, 2100 Martin Luther King, Jr. Avenue, SE, Washington, DC 20020; (202) 727-3688.

Florida. Check with the Florida Department of Education, 325 W Gaines Street, Tallahassee, FL 32399; (850) 245-0505.

Georgia. Records of public institutions are stored at a central location: Board of Regents of the University System of Georgia, 270 Washington Street, SW, Atlanta, GA 30334; (404) 656-2202. Records of schools converting from private to public status would be maintained by the newly created public institution. Religiously affiliated schools would make individual arrangements. Records for vocational/technical schools and proprietary institutions are maintained by Georgia State Department of Education, Atlanta, GA 30334.

Hawaii. Check with the State Postsecondary Education Commission, University of Hawaii, 2444 Dole Street, Honolulu, HI 96822; (808) 956-8207.

Illinois. Check with the Illinois Board of Higher Education, 4 W Old Capital Plaza, Room 500, Springfield, IL 62601; (217)

54

782-2551. See *www.isbe.net/pbvs/pdf/closed_ schools.pdf.*

Indiana. Records are stored at Indiana University at Bloomington and Indianapolis. Check also with the Indiana Commission for Higher Education, 101 W Ohio Street, Suite 550, Indianapolis, IN 46204; (317) 464-4400.

Iowa. Records are stored at a central location: The University of Iowa Registrar's Office, 1 Jessup Hall, Iowa City, IA 52242; (319) 335-0238.

Kansas. Records are stored at other institutions. Check also Kansas Board of Regents, 1000 SW Jackson St. Suite 520, Topeka, Kansas 66612-6813; (785) 296-3421. Also, to obtain a transcript from a closed school, visit *www.kansasregents.org/download.*

Kentucky. Records are stored at other institutions within the organization in control (*e.g.,* denomination for church school or institution assuming control). Check also with the Kentucky Council on Higher Education, 1024 Capital Center, Suite 320, Frankfort, KY 40601; (502) 573-1555.

Louisiana. Check with the Department of Education, Bureau of Student Services, Box 94064, Baton Rouge, LA 70804; (504) 342-4411.

Maine. Records for state institutions are stored at a central location: Department of Education Division of Higher Education Services, 23 State House Station, Augusta, ME 04333; (207) 624-6600. For directions on how to obtain a transcript from a closed institution visit www.maine.gov/education/ highered/Transcripts/Transcripts.htm.

Maryland. Records are stored at a central location: Maryland Higher Education Commission, 839 Bestgate Road, Suite 400, Annapolis, MD 21401; (410) 260-4500. For a list of closed schools visit *http://mhec. maryland.gov/career/pcs/index.asp.* It is possible also to make arrangements with the State Board of Higher Education to store records elsewhere.

Massachusetts. Records are stored at other institutions. Central directory is maintained by the Massachusetts Department of Higher Education, One Ashburton Place, Room 1401 McCormack Building, Boston, MA 02108; (617) 727-7785. See *www.mass. edu/forstudents/diplomas/closedinstlist.asp.*

Michigan. The Directory of Michigan Institutions of Higher Education is maintained by Michigan Department of Energy, Labor, and Economic Growth, The Division of Lifelong Learning, PO Box 30004, Lansing, MI 48909, (517) 373-8800. For a list of closed proprietary schools visit *www. michiganps.net/closed.aspx.*

Minnesota. Records are stored at other institutions. There is no central directory. Institutions that are closing make arrangements with another school to accommodate records. Check also with the Minnesota Higher Education Services Office, 400 Capitol Square Building, 550 Cedar Street, St. Paul, MN 55101; (612) 296-9665. For a list of closed schools visit *www.ohe.state. mn.us/sPagesOHE/closedSchoolContact.cfm.*

Mississippi. Check with the Board of Trustees of State Institutions of Higher Learning, 3825 Ridgewood Road, Jackson, MS

39211; (601) 432-6198. To request a transcript from a closed school visit *www.ihl.state.ms.us/oasa/mcca.html*.

Missouri. Inquiries about closed schools can be made by contacting the Missouri Department of Education, 3515 Amazonas Dr., Jefferson City, MO 65109; (573) 751-2361. For more information visit *www.dhe.mo.gov/closedschool.shtml*.

Montana. Records of state institutions are stored at a central location: Commissioner of Higher Education, 33 South Last Chance Gulch, Helena, MT 59601; (406) 444-6570. There is no policy covering private schools. Disposition of records would be made by the governing unit.

Nebraska. Records are stored in a central location: University of Nebraska–Lincoln, Registrar's Office, Lincoln, NE 68588; (402) 472-7211.

Nevada. Records are stored in a central location: Nevada Commission on Postsecondary Education, 1000 East Williams, Room 120, Carson City, NV 89710; (702) 885-5690.

New Hampshire. Records are stored in a central location: New Hampshire Postsecondary Education Commission, 3 Barrell Court, Suite 300, Concord, NH 03301. For more information visit *www.nh.gov/postsecondary/closed/closed_c_u.html*.

New Jersey. Records are stored at other institutions. Schools make their own arrangements. Check also the Commission on Higher Education, 20 West State Street, 7th Floor, Trenton, NJ 08608-1206; (609) 292-4310; See *www.nj.gov/highereducation/colleges/closed_renamed.htm*.

New Mexico. Check with the New Mexico Higher Education Department, 2048 Galisteo St., Santa Fe, NM 87505; (505) 476-8400. For more information and a list of closed schools visit *http://hed.state.nm.us/content.asp?CustComKey=193250&CategoryKey=195545&pn=Page&DomName=hed.state.nm.us*.

New York. In some cases the State Education Department takes over records: New York State Education Department, Office of Higher Education, State Education Building - 2nd floor West Mezzanine, Albany, NY 12234; (518) 474-3862. For a list of closed schools visit *www.highered.nysed.gov/ocue/spr/closedInstDirectory.htm*.

North Carolina. Records are stored in a central location: Division of Archives and History, State of North Carolina, 215 North Blount Street, Raleigh, NC 27601; (919) 735-3952. Check also with the Commission on Higher Education Facilities, UNC General Administration, 910 Raleigh Road, PO Box 2688, Chapel Hill, NC 27515; (919) 549-8614.

North Dakota. Check with the North Dakota University System, State Capitol, Tenth Floor, 600 E Boulevard Avenue, Bismarck, ND 58505; (701) 328-4114.

Ohio. Check with the Ohio Board of Regents, 30 E Broad Street, Columbus, OH 43266; (614) 466-7420.

Oklahoma. Records are stored at other institutions. Check also with the Oklahoma State Regents for Higher Education, 655 Research Parkway, Suite 200, Oklahoma City, OK 73104; (405) 225-9100. For a list of closed institutions visit *www.okhighered. org/student-center/college-stdnts/academic/ transcripts.shtml.*

Oregon. Check with the Oregon State Board of Higher Education, PO Box 3175, Eugene, OR 97403; (514) 346-5795.

Pennsylvania. Check with the Pennsylvania Department of Education, 333 Market Street, Twelfth Floor, Harrisburg, PA 17126; (717) 783-6788. For a list of closed schools visit *www.portal.state.pa.us/portal/server.pt/ community/private_licensed_schools/8993/ closed_school_records/530978.*

Rhode Island. Records are stored at other institutions. There is no central directory. Check also with the Office of Higher Education, 301 Promenade Street, Providence, RI 02908; (401) 222-6561.

South Carolina. Check with The South Carolina Commission on Higher Education, 1333 Main Street, Suite 200, Columbia, SC; (803) 737-2260.

Tennessee. There is no central depository or directory. Check with the Tennessee Higher Education Commission, Parkway Towers, Suite 1900, 404 James Robertson Parkway, Nashville, TN 37243; (615) 741-3605. For more information visit *www.state.tn.us/ thec/Divisions/LRA/PostsecondaryAuth/ academic_transcripts.html.*

Texas. Records are stored at other institutions. There is no central directory. Each institution makes its own decision. State archives will store state agencies' records, but it is not required. Check also with the Texas Higher Education Coordinating Board, Capitol Station, PO Box 17688, Austin, TX 78711; (512) 483-6101 or the Texas Workforce Commission, 101 E. 15th St. Room 651, Austin, TX 78778; (512) 427-6200.

Utah. Check with the Utah State Board of Regents, Board of Regents Building, The Gateway, 60 South 400 West, Salt Lake City, UT 84101; (801) 321-7103.

Vermont. Records are stored at a central location: Office of the Secretary of State, 1078 U.S. Route 2, Montpelier, VT 05633; (802) 828-3700.

Virginia. Check with the State Council of Higher Education for Virginia; www.schev. edu/ClosedInstitutions.aspx; 101 N. 14th St., James Monroe Building, Richmond, VA 23219; (804) 225-2600.

Washington. Regionally nonaccredited institutions must file records with the Higher Education Coordinating Board, 917 Lakeridge Way, Olympia, WA 98504; (360) 753-7800. Regionally accredited institutions may make individual arrangements with other institutions. There is no central directory. See *www.hecb.wa.gov/autheval/ daa/ClosedSchoolsTranscripts.asp.*

West Virginia. Check with the West Virginia Higher Education Policy Commission, 1018 Kanawha Boulevard East, Suite 700, Charleston, WV 25301; (304) 558-2101.

Wisconsin. Records are stored at other institutions. Check also with the State of Wisconsin Educational Approval Board, 30 W. Mifflin St., 9th Floor, PO Box 8696, Madison, WI 53708; (608) 266-1996. See *http:// eab.state.wi.us/resources/closedschools.asp.*

Wyoming. No closings are reported but policies for private schools would require the parent institution to retain records. State institutions would probably be covered by state policy requiring either the Department of Education or State Archives to be responsible for records that are probably microfilmed and stored at a central location in Cheyenne. Check also with the Wyoming Community College Commission, 2020 Carey, 8th Floor, Cheyenne, WY 82002; (307) 777-7763.

State Records Management/ Archive Web Sites

TABLE II

State	Dept	URL
Alabama	Alabama Department of Archives and History, State Records Center (ADAH)	www.archives.alabama.gov/ officials/rec-center.html
Alaska	Alaska State Archives	www.archives.state.ak.us/records_ management/records_management.html
Arizona	Arizona State Library, Archives, and Public Records- Records Management Division	www.lib.az.us/records/
Arkansas	Arkansas History Commission (AHC)	www.ark-ives.com/
California	California Records and Information Management (CalRIM) and State Records Center (SRC)	www.osp.dgs.ca.gov/recsctr/default.htm
Colorado	Colorado State Archives- Records Management Services	www.colorado.gov/dpa/doit/archives/rm/
Connecticut	Connecticut State Library- Office of the Public Records Administrator (OPRA)	www.cslib.org/publicrecords/
Delaware	Delaware Public Archives	http://archives.delaware.gov/ aboutagency.shtml
Florida	Florida Department of State- State Library and Archives of Florida	http://dlis.dos.state.fl.us/index_researchers.cfm
Georgia	Georgia Archives- Records and Information Management Services	http://sos.georgia.gov/archives/ who_are_we/rims/default.htm
Hawaii	State Records Center	http://hawaii.gov/dags/archives/ records-management

TABLE II

State	Dept	URL
Idaho	State Record Center Services	http://adm.idaho.gov/purchasing/record_cnt.htm
Illinois	Illinois State Archives	www.cyberdriveillinois.com/departments/archives/archives.html
Indiana	Indiana Commission on Public Records	www.in.gov/icpr/2361.htm
Iowa	State Records Commission	www.iowasrc.org/
Kansas	Kansas State Historical Society-Records Management	www.kshs.org/government/records/recordsmanagement.htm
Kentucky	Kentucky Department for Libraries and Archives	www.kdla.ky.gov/home.htm
Louisiana	Louisiana State Records Center	www.sos.louisiana.gov/tabid/492/Default.aspx
Maine	Maine State Archives- State Agency Records	www.maine.gov/sos/arc/records/homepage.html
Maryland	Department of General Services-Procurement & Logistics	www.dgs.maryland.gov/overview/logistics.htm
Massachusetts	State Records Center	www.sec.state.ma.us/rec/recabt/abtidx.htm
Michigan	Records Management Services	www.michigan.gov/recordsmanagement/
Minnesota	Minnesota State Archives	www.mnhs.org/preserve/records/gov_services.htm
Mississippi	Mississippi Department of Archives and History (MDAH)-State Government Records Office	http://mdah.state.ms.us/recman/recmntxt.php
Missouri	Secretary of State State Records Management	www.sos.mo.gov/records/recmgmt/
Montana	Secretary of State Records and Information Management Division	http://sos.mt.gov/Records/index.asp
Nebraska	Secretary of State Records Management Division	www.sos.ne.gov/dyindex.html#boxingName
Nevada	State Library and Archives Records Management Division	http://nevadaculture.org/nsla/index.php?option=com_content&task=view&id=503&Itemid=86
New Hampshire	Archives and Records Management	www.sos.nh.gov/archives/stateagencies.html
New Jersey	Division of Archives and Records Management	www.njarchives.org/links/recman.html
New Mexico	Commission of Public Records ~ State Records Center and Archives	www.nmcpr.state.nm.us/
New York	State Archives and Records Administration	www.archives.nysed.gov/a/records/index.shtml
North Carolina	Information Technology Services	www.its.state.nc.us/ServiceCatalog/ElectronicDocumentManagementandProjectCollaboration.asp
North Dakota	North Dakota Information Technology Department Records Management	www.nd.gov/itd/records/

TABLE II

State	Dept	URL
Ohio	Records Management	www.das.ohio.gov/Divisions/GeneralServices/ StatePrintingandMailServices/ RecordsManagement/tabid/265/Default.aspx
Oklahoma	State Archives and Records Management Divisions	www.odl.state.ok.us/oar/index2.htm
Oregon	Oregon State Archives	http://arcweb.sos.state.or.us/recmgmt/ sched/gen/schoolmenu.html
Pennsylvania	Pennsylvania Office of Administration Records Management	www.portal.state.pa.us/portal/server. pt?open=514&objID=545577&mode=2
South Carolina	South Carolina Archives and Records Management	http://arm.scdah.sc.gov/
South Dakota	South Dakota State Archives	www.sdhistory.org/arc/archives.htm
Tennessee	Tennessee State Library and Archives	http://tn.gov/tsla/
Texas	Texas State Library and Archives Commission	www.tsl.state.tx.us/slrm/recordspubs/rrs3.html
Utah	Division of Archives and Records Service	http://archives.utah.gov/ recordsmanagement/index.html
Vermont	Vermont Secretary of State Archives and Records Administration	http://vermont-archives.org/ records/schedules/index.htm
Virginia	Library of Virginia Records Management	www.lva.virginia.gov/agencies/ records/sched_local/index.htm
Washington	Information Services Board Records Retention	http://isb.wa.gov/tools/webguide/records.aspx
West Virginia	West Virginia Office of Technology	www.technology.wv.gov/it-community/Pages/ WVRecordsManagementProcedures.aspx
Wisconsin	Department of Administration, Division of Enterprise Operations	www.doa.state.wi.us/subcategory. asp?linksubcatid=427&locid=2
Wyoming	Wyoming State Archives Records Management	http://wyoarchives.state.wy.us/ RecMan/index.asp

Glossary

Academic Record. The academic record is a chronological history of a student's entire quantitative and qualitative learning achievement and reflects the basis on which the individual entered and left the institution.

Administrative Value. The usefulness of records to the agency of origin for carrying on its day-to-day activities.

Archives. 1) The institution or facility for the permanent preservation of noncurrent records which are of permanent evidential or informational value for administrative, fiscal, historical, legal, or research purposes; 2) the holdings of that institution or facility.

Audit. An examination to ensure accuracy, compliance or accountability of access or data.

Authentication. The process of determining whether someone or something is, in fact, who or what it is declared to be in order to access information.

CCD (Charge-Coupled Device). Used in digital cameras and scanners to detect different light intensities and store the information.

CD-ROM (Compact Disc Read Only Memory). A compact disk that can only be read. All data to be stored on the disc is moved at one time; nothing can be added after the disc goes through its final burn process.

CMOS. Complementary metaloxide semiconductor used for application specific chips. It is in every PC bought and has been adapted to sense light.

COLD (Computer Output to Laser Disk). Information from reports, such as enrollment records, grades, reports, and w-2 forms, can be moved directly from a student information system to the COLD system without ever generating a paper copy.

Continuity Plan. Plan defining the steps required to restore business or system processes following a disruption in service.

Data. Representations of facts or concepts that can be communicated, interpreted, or processed by human or automatic means. Technically, data are the discrete units of information that the computer manipulates.

Data Custodian. University unit or employee responsible for the operation and management of systems and servers which collect, manage, and provide access to institutional data.

Data Integrity. Allows for accurate and complete data that is achieved by preventing unauthorized modification or destruction of data or databases.

Destruction of Records. Destruction of records means that all copies of the record in all media be destroyed.

Documentation. An organized body of information needed to plan, develop, operate, maintain, and use machine-readable records and automated systems. Datafile documentation is used to explain the arrangement, contents, and coding of the information in a machine-readable file.

DVD (Digital Versatile Disk or Digital Video Disk). Type of CD-ROM technology with the potential to store over 25 times as much information as traditional CD-ROMs.

EDMS (Electronic Document Management System). A type of software that is designed for the organizing, filing, retrieving, and distribution of any type of electronic files (images, sounds, documents, etc.)

Hard Copy. Information printed on paper or other durable surface such as microfilm. This term is used to distinguish printed information from the temporary image represented on a CRT screen, and from the machine-readable information on a magnetic tape, disk, or diskette, or in the computer's main memory.

Hardware-Dependent. Any machine-readable file that requires one particular make or model of computer or peripheral equipment is hardware-dependent (also called machine-dependent). Machine-readable records that can be used on any computer are machine or hardware-independent.

Historical Value. The usefulness of records for historical research concerning the agency of origin or for information about persons, places, events, or things.

Inventory. A descriptive listing, by series, of the records of an agency or administrative unit, including information on records titles, purposes or uses, contents, types and formats, frequency of reference, volumes, dates, arrangements and locations.

Jukebox. Device attached to an imaging system that holds multiple optical disks and is programmed to select one when prompted.

Machine-Readable. Information in a form that can be processed only directly by a computer, usually in the form of magnetic or electronic impulses.

Non-Record Materials. (1) Published or duplicated material which is neither created nor received by an agency in the course of conducting its business, which is of no evidential or informational value in documenting an agency's policy, history, or official business or in substantiating legal rights or obligations, but which is collected and retained for reference use only; (2) ephemera, such as notes, created for immediate use only and not maintained in compliance with statutory requirements.

Optical Disk. A storage device which utilizes reflecting surfaces, photographic processes, or photochromic processes to read and write data on a disk. Usually a laser beam is employed to burn tiny pits on the surface of the disk. The pits reflect light when a read laser is focused on them.

Record. Any book, paper, map, photograph, film, recording, or other document or any copy thereof, regardless of physical medium, format, type or characteristic, created or received by an agency or its officers or employees in connection with the transaction of public business and retained by that agency or its successor as evidence of its activities or functions or because of the information it contains about those activities or functions.

Records Disposition. The action or actions taken, or scheduled to be taken, to deal with records, including retention in office of origin; destruction; transfer to a records center; microform reproduction prior to destruction; transfer to an archive for permanent preservation.

Records Disposition Authorization. Legal authorization, by the Archives and Records Commission, for the disposition, on a single occasion, of a particular body of records which are not subject to the continuing authority of a Records Disposition Schedule.

Records Disposition Schedule. A schedule, approved by the Archives and Records Commission, authorizing, on a continuing basis, the respective disposition of each of several of an agency's or administrative unit's records series, following a designated period of retention, by the agency or administrative unit, of each series.

Records Management. A program designed to enable and facilitate maximum economy and efficiency in the creation, organization, maintenance, use, and disposition of records, assuring that useful records will be preserved as long as needed and that needless records will not be created or preserved beyond their usefulness.

Record Series. Documents, volumes, folders, reels, or other units of the same record title arranged under a single filing system or kept together as a unit because they relate to a particular subject, result from the same activity, or have a particular form.

Research Value. The usefulness of records for research by government, business or other private organizations and scholars.

Retention Period. The scheduled period of time for retention of a records series.

Schedule. *See* Records Disposition Schedule.

Security Breach. Any action that results in the unauthorized access, alteration, destruction or disclosure of University information, or information systems, or the dissemination of information/data to unauthorized individuals or parties.

Security Measures. Processes, software and/or hardware used by system and network administrators to assure confidentiality, integrity and availability of computers, networks and data belonging to the university and users of university computer and network resources. Security measures include the ability to review files for potential or actual policy violations and responsibility for investigation of security related issues.

Security Violations. Any action that does not comply with system security concepts, policies, processes, procedures or measures.

Series. *See* Records Series.

Source Documents. Documents containing information entered into a computer.

Storage Media. The materials on which data are written and stored. Examples include punchcards, magnetic tape, disks, diskettes, and drums.

Student Records. Student records are those created to assist the Offices of Admissions, Financial Aid, Records, or the Registrar in their support of basic institutional objectives and include any records with students' names: files, documents, and materials in whatever medium, which contain information that identifies a person.

TIFF IV (Tagged Image File Format). A standard created by CCITT (International Consultative Committee for Telegraphy and Telephony, a French standardizing group) in 1984 for compressing black and white images at a ratio of 15:5.

Type of Records. The functional category of a record, such as correspondence, directive, report, payroll, requisition, purchase order, invoice, minutes of proceedings, inventory, receipt, contact, voucher, warrant, case file, budget, statement of account, application, time card, ledger, court order, map, plat, drawing, etc.

WORM (Write Once, Read Many). Any technology that uses lasers to create changes in a CD-like platter to be written once and read over and over again.

Useful References

American Association of Collegiate Registrars and Admissions Officers. 2003. *Academic Record and Transcript Guide*. Washington, DC: AACRAO.

———. 2006a. *The AACRAO 2006 FERPA Guide*. Washington, DC: AACRAO.

———. 2006b. *The Registrar's Guide: Evolving Best Practices in Records and Registration*. Washington, DC: AACRAO.

———. 2009. *Transfer Credit Practices of Designated Educational Institutions*. Washington, DC: AACRAO.

American Association of Collegiate Registrars and Admissions Officers and CAUSE. 1997. *Privacy and the Handling of Student Information in the Electronic Networked Environments of Colleges and Universities*. Denver, CO: AACRAO and CAUSE.

Association for Information and Image Management. *Standards for Micrographics*.

Barriff, Marjorie Rabe. 1996. The appraisal of personally identifiable student records. *American Archivist*. 49(3): 263–275.

Byrne, Tony. 2006. Content management: Twelve implementation pitfalls to avoid. *Inside Knowledge*. September 11. Available at: <www.ikmagazine.com/xq/asp/txtSearch.Taxonomies/exactphrase.1/sid.0/articleid.6A01811E-0DEB-4896-858A-DD4E76B4284D/qx/display.htm>

"Computer output microfilm." A Dictionary of Business and Management. 2006. Retrieved December 15, 2009 from: <www.encyclopedia.com/doc/1O18-computeroutputmicrofilm.html>.

Educational Amendments of 1976 (PL 94482), Title IV, Part F. Subpart 1, Section 493A(a)(1) (20 USC 1088 b1).

Federal Interagency Committee on Education. 1978. *Keeping Your School or College Catalog in Compliance with Federal Laws and Regulations*.

Geller, Sidney B. 1983. *Care and Handling of Computer Magnetic Storage Media*. NBS Computer Science and Technology Special Publication No. 500101. U. S. Department of Commerce, National Bureau of Standards. Washington, DC: US Government Printing Office.

Guymon, Fred E. 1986. *National and International Records Retention Standards*.

Hedstrom, Margaret L. 1984. *Archives and Manuscripts: Machine-Readable Records*. Society of American Archivists.

Higher Education Act of 1965 (PL 89329). Higher Education Amendments of 1998 Student Assistance General Provisions 34 CFR 668.

Hyman, Ursula H. 1982. The family educational rights and privacy act of 1974 and the college record systems of the future. *Computer Law Journal*. 3(Summer): 583–618.

Marks, Donald D. 1983. AACRAO's guide for retention and disposal of student records: A critical review. *Midwestern Archivist*. 8(1): 27–33.

Patten, B. 1985. Source document microfilm exposed. *Journal of information and Image Management*.

Peterson, Gary M., and Trudy Huskamp Peterson. 1985. *Archives and Manuscripts: Law*. Society of American Archivists.

Piechowski, John. 2009. Ten important things to consider before you buy a CMS: A presentation. *Avoiding CMS Pitfalls*. Feb 17. Available at <http://learn.northwoodsoft.com/Milwaukee-Past-Sessions/Seminar-Avoiding-CMS-Pitfalls.htm>.

Society of American Archivists. 1979. *College and University Archives. Selected Readings*.

U. S. Department of Education. Family Educational Rights and Privacy Act (FERPA), 20 USC, 1231g; *See also* 34 CFR 99.

Veterans' Education and Employment Act of 1976 (PL 94502).